A MUDDY LIFE

*A Mom and Son's Differing Perspectives
on Living with Cerebral Palsy*

RUTH GRANT-BAILEY

For my son, Mason Bailey,
who co-wrote this book with me.
I loved how you shared your differing opinions with me and the
world. You have broadened my awareness and enriched my life,
in more ways than one!

For Rick, Leah, and Quinn, thank you for tolerating Mason's and
my shenanigans. You three are the wind beneath our wings.

Ruth

Dedicated to those who see me, hear me,
love me unconditionally and understand me.
I am grateful for my life...just the way it is!

Mason

Contents

Preface

Hi, my name is Ruth Grant-Bailey, I am the mother of four beautiful, perfect children: Leah, Mason, Jackson (angel baby), and Quinn. I appreciate you reading our story and hope you will gain some strength, inspiration, knowledge, or at a minimum, enjoy a laugh or two as Mason and I share our experience with him having been born with cerebral palsy.

***

Hi, my name is Mason. I am twenty-five years old at the time of this writing, and it is my immense pleasure to share my own take on being born and raised with cerebral palsy. My mom is the most incredible mom! She has been my rock and helped me pave my way through roadblocks, over hurdles, and around steep mountains, but sometimes even her perspective is different than mine. I could not share my thoughts at an early age, and even into my older years some things were scary to share even with her.

Let's start with the title of this book, "A Muddy Life." From my mom's perspective, it means things were not always smooth and neat raising me, but for me, muddy means living my best life! The muddier I am, the happier I am. I love to be outside, get dirty, and play in the mud.

I hope you find some solace in knowing that things are not always as they seem. I hope you realize you are stronger than you know. And most importantly, I want you to know life is an Earthly lesson and a chance to learn and grow regardless of our abilities or disabilities.

You Do Not Know What
You Do Not Know

It is amazing what you do not know you do not know.

My husband Rick and I met in college. We were set up by our friends on a blind date. That simple introduction was the trajectory of our lifetime together!

Our relationship began in 1989 and was full of love, laughter, and happiness. We enjoyed each other's company and just had fun as we made our way through college. Rick and I got engaged in 1991 and bought our first house in a quaint neighborhood. It was a cute ranch that backed up to the local elementary school.

Rick is an avid walker. He has walked and continues to walk daily to this day. He uses walking to clear his mind and get physical exercise. He has also used it to entertain our youngsters and train our dogs over the years.

I like to walk, but not all the time. I'm the type of walker where the weather must be such and such, I must be in the mood, and the timing has to be right.

Over the first year or so, when I would venture out with Rick on a walk, I would see a mother pushing an enormous wheelchair carrying her daughter, who I assume was approximately fourteen years of age. The girl was bundled up from top to bottom with

1

gear. Even if the weather was nice, she would have a blanket over her. The chair was tilted back, and there was equipment attached to the wheelchair.

As we passed, I would hear the girl moan, shriek, and let out incomprehensible sounds. The mother would respond back lovingly and happily. They daughter's legs and her spine were curved. She had a bib on to catch the accumulation of drool.

Sharing this is not a proud moment for me, but I want to be honest, transparent, and real. Passing this mother and her daughter put thoughts in my head of sadness and despair.

I felt sorry for the mother.

I felt sorry for the child.

I remember thinking, What's wrong with her? What happened to her? That poor girl and poor mom.

I remember thinking there was no way that child knew what was going on.

At that time, I had no idea what cerebral palsy was. Okay, I take that back. I knew cerebral palsy was brain damage. Brain damage to me, back then, meant intellectual deficits, cognitive impairment, physical disability, and hardship. To me, it meant a life of being cared for, not knowing what was going on, a limitation of abilities, and not being a "true part" of community. Although my heart went out to them, I was uneducated, and I was uncomfortable. Since I was uncomfortable, I would not make eye contact or speak to either one of them.

At the time of this encounter, I was enrolled in nursing school. It dawned on me that nursing school had not taught us anything regarding disabilities. I remember thinking to myself, I wonder when that education will come.

It never did.

As I write this, I'm still horrified by my behavior. I'm mad as hell at myself. I wish I could go back and say "Hello" and start a conversation with that bundled-up adorable young lady and her precious mom. I wish I could apologize to them for my younger, ignorant self. If it were today, I guarantee our interactions would land in a forever friendship of love, empathy, and support.

***

Ha! My mom didn't realize that the Universe was putting things into motion for her back in 1991. Circumstances, relationships, and experiences take you where you need to be at any given time in your life. Those walks and seeing that girl and her mom was the beginning of preparing her and my dad for my future.

There are no coincidences. Too many things must align for things to happen as they do. The Divine knew what it was doing, and I trust in the journey that was made for me.

Those simple encounters on those neighborhood walks were sparking my mom's thought processes. Why would my mom have known what cerebral palsy was? She had no experience with it. She'd had no encounters with it (other than this one, which she bombed). She was not given any education about it. She only knew what she knew—cerebral palsy meant brain damage.

And, as unfortunate as it is, judgment and forming of opinions come with lack of knowledge. I hate to say it, but this is just how the world works. Judgment starts with thoughts of incapableness, unworthiness, and placement of limitations.

Discomfort is what can change energy. It is the tool that will fuel you, educate you, and change you. It is in discomfort that one must decide to learn and grow or walk away from it. In 1991, my mom walked away from her discomfort. Even with her walking away, it made her aware.

Change starts there—being aware.

As far as nursing school is concerned, she was on to something. The medical field is not equipped or prepared for those of us with disabilities, even today. Medical professionals are uncomfortable because they have not been exposed to or taught how to treat people who have disabilities. They are taught to manage diagnoses, promote health, prevent disease, or provide treatment. All of these things are good, but they do not always help those of us challenged with a disability because our challenges are interwoven. For example, you will read later how the orthopedic surgeon wanted to fix my bone because it was bowing but when asked how it would affect my walk (neurologically) he wasn't sure. That is a problem for someone who would like to continue to walk!

Like my mom, physicians and healthcare personnel lack education, exposure, and experience. As I tell the medical residents I speak to at our local university, people with cerebral palsy or another disability are not scary! I also tell them, "Now is the time to learn and understand what living with a disability is like, so ask me anything."

You do not know what you do not know!

Their Uncertainty Is My Happiness

On February 6, 1993, we began our journey together as husband and wife. It was a journey that would test us as a couple, challenge us as a family, and question our union. I'm not sure either of us would have signed the marriage license that day had we known what we were in for. But I can honestly say I would not have wanted to do life with anyone else besides Rick. I am so grateful for him, his support, his involvement, and his unconditional love for me and our family.

Three years into our marriage, we decided it was time to start our family. The thought of having a baby was incredibly exciting, but also scary at the same time. Throughout our pregnancy, especially after the ultrasound declared the baby a boy, we were in bliss over having our first child.

We could not wait to meet "Mason." Everything about "Mason" was easy. I got pregnant as soon as we tried; I was able to work as a nurse through the whole pregnancy; I took college classes for my bachelor's degree, vacationed, and lived life the same as before I was pregnant.

The only difficulty I recall with having "Mason" was "he" was NOT on time. Ten days after my due date, the obstetrician said it was time to be induced. Nineteen hours after induction, SHE was delivered vaginally at a whopping nine pounds, eight ounces!

On September 24, 1996, our time as a childless couple ended with the birth of our beautiful daughter, Leah McKayla Bailey.

Hearing "It's a girl!" shocked every person in the delivery room! The ultrasound, or the technician who read the ultrasound, was wrong. No one cared about the gender—we just wanted the baby to be healthy—but to hear "girl" after thinking and planning for a "boy" was confusing and exciting.

My mom, my in-laws, and my husband all witnessed the miraculous birth of Leah. She was perfect! Although she was on the larger size for a baby, there wasn't a flaw to be seen. Not only was this the beginning of Rick's and my family, but this was also the start of unconditional and extravagant love. A love we didn't understand or even know was possible until she was placed in our arms.

Leah continued her easy ways in our lives. She was sleeping through the night by six weeks old. She developed a routine and stuck to it consistently with naps, feedings, and activities. She went with the flow as we went to well visits, family outings, and other activities.

She was just so easy.

If it was said to us once, it was said a hundred times: "You are lucky. Babies are not usually this good and this easy. Do not expect the next one to be."

Ha! Next one?

We were not thinking about a next one at that point. We continued our life as a family of three. Leah was smart as a whip, caught onto things quickly, and was so sweet. She was caring beyond her age, and Mommy's little helper.

She and I enjoyed every single day. I would volunteer at her preschool. We would arrange playdates with her friends at parks, go to the pool, and have picnics. We enjoyed our daily naps together. We laughed, sang, read, and played.

I remember the thrill I got when I would sign cards, "Ruth, Rick, and Leah."

It's hard to explain the love a mother and child have to those who have not experienced it. As I cradled, played with, and took care of that precious little girl, when I looked into her eyes, she was an extension of my heart.

***

Love.

Babies are pure divinity! Pure love.

When babies are born, the babies are the only ones crying; no one else in the room is. Everyone else is joyful, happy, and excited. The baby is crying because they are leaving a place of unconditional love and acceptance.

As people get older and die, everyone surrounding them is crying and the person dying is not. This is because the person dying knows they are going to a place of unconditional love and acceptance, and they are not sad about that.

We must remember the beauty and where we came from. We come from light and love and will return to light and love.

Everyone seeks love. Unconditional love. We are all born deserving of love.

Inhale light, exhale love!

***

When Leah was three years old, Rick and I thought it was time to expand our family. We were in a good routine, Leah would be starting preschool, and it just felt right. It was time to give her a sibling and increase our family to four!

As strange as this sounds, I knew exactly when I became pregnant the second time. The morning after a specific night of making love, I knew when I took the pregnancy test that month it would clearly show two lines. Call it intuition, motherly knowledge, or just a hunch, but I was correct; my next pregnancy test had two neon pink lines that could be seen from across the room. Our family would be growing!

Six weeks into our pregnancy, I was working at a local hospital on night shift as a registered nurse in Cincinnati. During the shift I took a potty break, and upon wiping I noticed blood on the tissue. My heart sank and sadness filled me to the core. I was certain this was the start of a miscarriage. After my shift was over, I made an appointment with my obstetrician.

At the appointment she recommended an ultrasound, which was scheduled at the hospital, not done in the office. Rick and I went to the ultrasound scared, unsure what we were going to be told. We were expecting the worst. I remember the initial relief hearing the whoosh, whoosh, whoosh sound coming from the ultrasound machine.

A heartbeat.

Thank you! Thank you!

Then, these words from the ultrasound technician: "Well, I think I know why you had some bleeding."

My heart slowed back down to an almost non-existent beat. What was she going to say? No one in that room expected, or was prepared, to hear what came next.

"You're having twins!"

What the what? How is this even possible? I mean I know how it works and how it's possible, but not for us! We didn't have a family history of twins. We didn't use in-vitro or anything like that, and we certainly didn't plan to grow our family twofold.

Rick's face! You would have thought he'd seen a ghost! Eyes big, mouth open, unable to speak.

The tech explained that implantation, especially with twins, can cause spotting, thus the reason I had a blood-tinged wipe when I used the restroom at work.

After we both caught our breath, our laughter turned into tears, and we embraced each other. As the shock subsided, the excitement emerged. We were going to do this! We were going to raise two beautiful babies at the same time (or so we thought), along with our precious daughter.

Our extended family, especially the grandparents, were out of their minds with anticipation.

Twins? Really?

Rick and I started planning. We started having conversations about raising two babies and the challenges it would bring (double diaper duty, double costs, college tuition for two, etc.). However, our worries and uncertainties were surpassed by happiness, excitement, and the love we were experiencing times two.

It was surreal! One of the biggest highs of our lives!

That was until . . . we had our first appointment following the ultrasound.

The obstetrician, who we will call Dr. Maggie, confirmed, "Yes, you are having twins." Then she elaborated with, "Everyone gets so excited and happy about having twins, but what they don't realize is carrying two babies doubles the risk for complications."

I remember thinking WTH! That thought lasted for about two seconds, then I didn't think about her statement again until . . . six weeks later, maybe?

My pregnancy continued. We were still extremely early, eight to ten weeks at that point. The spotting had stopped, as they predicted it would, since the embryos had successfully implanted into my uterine wall. The next stage of pregnancy was genetic testing.

Genetic testing included blood work that could show risk factors for things like Down syndrome, cystic fibrosis, etc. Checking for these genetic disorders is totally optional. The medical team asked if this was something we wanted to have done.

It was a hard decision because, for us, it wouldn't change a damn thing. But as a control freak, planner, and nurse, and in the best interest of our babies, I wanted to proceed with the testing so we could either breathe a little easier or prepare for what we may have to deal with.

A few days after I had completed the bloodwork, I received a phone call. I remember that phone call clearly. I was in the kitchen. Back then landline phones were still used regularly. Our phone hung on the wall, and I picked up the receiver and said, "Hello?"

"Ruth? Hi, this is Dr. Maggie, I am calling about the results of your bloodwork."

At first my heart skipped a beat, but then I calmed my mind instantly with the thought: She is just calling because I'm a nurse, and she is being professional about it instead of waiting for a visit.

She continued, "Do you want to come into the office to go over the results or would you like me to explain them to you on the phone?"

She had my full-blown attention. "Uh . . . please tell me now on the phone," I whispered into the receiver.

"Ruth, unfortunately, your blood work came back indicating there is a very high risk of your babies having Down syndrome."

Silence. I felt a pit in my stomach. Thoughts shut down. I was unable to speak. Finally, I was able to mutter "Okay."

Dr. Maggie explained the test was not a definitive one. It was merely an indicator, and to have a definitive answer would require testing of the amniotic fluid. Aspiration of amniotic fluid does not come without risks. Obtaining amniotic fluid could cause premature labor. It could cause complications to the babies in utero.

She concluded, "Please think things over, discuss this with your husband, and let me know what you want to do at your next appointment."

I slowly placed the receiver back into the wall mount. I walked over to the dining room chair to sit down. I laid my head on the table, not knowing what to think.

I, honestly, was emotionless. Two babies with Down syndrome? How will I be able to handle this with a three-year-old? What does this even mean? What kind of things will I have to do for these babies?

OMG!

A thought presented itself and consumed me: Babies who have Down syndrome often are born with heart defects and require open-heart surgery. Two babies having open-heart surgery?

My inner thoughts continued to race.

I don't know if I can do this! What choice do I have?

Of course, you can do this. You're their mother!

You're a registered nurse, for crying out loud!

My inner dialogue fought back. A nurse. That is a job, not day-to-day life.

I have an ongoing joke that says, "I do not nurse at home unless there is blood." Of course, everyone knows I am just kidding. But now it was not a joke. I was going to be caring for two babies and a three-year-old. Two babies with medical and mental challenges at the same time for the rest of my life.

I did not sign up for or agree to this!

Good ole Dr. Maggie's words haunted me: "Two babies bring twice the complications."

ERRRGH!!!!

Pissed! I WAS PISSED! Anger seethed in me. I felt, in that moment, I just could not handle this outcome.

Rick is so patient, so kind, so understanding, and my rock. Sometimes these characteristics can be at his expense as he internalizes his emotions just to be brave and strong for others; in this case, me.

In my angry, emotional, scared state, I relayed to him the call from Dr. Maggie.

In his reasonable, calm, logical manner, he said, "Honey, first, it is not definitive at this point. She said it would require further testing. Yes, it seems like the blood sample indicates a high risk, but we cannot assume and say something is something when we do not have all the information in front of us." He continued. "Second, we can do this. We will love our babies and take care of them, no matter what! It is going to be okay; I promise."

And with that he grabbed and hugged me as tears gushed down my cheeks.

Silence entered our relationship. We did not talk about the situation. At the time, I don't think the phone call bothered Rick. He is a very analytical person and data is in his blood. Therefore, in his mind, this was only a possibility, and he was waiting for the actual results.

However, me being a nurse, I saw the babies born with Down syndrome being rushed to the local children's hospital for open-heart surgery immediately following delivery. I envisioned Rick and I at the hospital with our two babies being airlifted to the neonatal intensive care unit for their surgery . . . alone. It was a mental war, with my thoughts full of worse case scenarios minute after minute, hour after hour, day after day.

My next OB appointment was a few days away.

"Rick, we need to talk. We need to decide whether to do the next phase of testing on the babies. Do we want a definitive answer, knowing that it could put the babies at risk, and even me if I went into premature labor?"

Rick, with the sweetness in his heart and eyes, looked at me and said, "Honey, it's up to you and what you need to know. I am fine either way."

Help!

Why am I the emotional one?

Why am I the over-thinker?

I do not know what the fuck to do or decide!

This decision is bigger than me!

UGH!

Help me!

Please.

We finally decided the definitive testing was not in the best interest of the babies, or me. The OB had explained that characteristics of Down syndrome can often be seen on ultrasounds as the babies grow, including heart defects, thickened nuchal fold, and long bone shortening. So, we opted at that appointment not to have amniotic fluid aspirated to test for a definitive diagnosis. We would let the upcoming ultrasounds help us gain knowledge.

As weeks and months went by, I began to accept that I was having twins who would be born with Down syndrome. I started doing online research, as much as I could. It is not pleasurable reading things and then envisioning them affecting your unborn children. But I wanted to know as much as I could so I could be prepared and be a good mother to my children.

When I was around twenty weeks along in the pregnancy, we were scheduled for another ultrasound. This one would show any discrepancies in growth, any markers for Down syndrome, and any heart concerns. It was also the ultrasound where we would find out the gender of the children. At least these were all the things we thought we would be finding out!

Laying on the table, shirt pulled up, stomach large and exposed, I heard the technician say those magic words: "This gel is going to be cold."

The gel was applied. The wand was placed on my belly, smearing the gel around to begin the process of showing us our babies in utero. It is one of the coolest technologies there is. The ability to see your children's heart beating and to see their extremities moving is simply amazing!

"Mr. and Mrs. Bailey, you are having twin boys!"

Oh, the tears began flowing, not only from my eyes, but Rick's as well.

Boys! Two boys!

Of course, jokes were made in the room, "You have the start of your own football team." "They'll be able to play pickle instead of just tossing the baseball with Dad."

The excitement and happiness were immediately halted as the technician said, "Now, let's start getting some measurements."

My nurse hat went on, and my healthcare ears perked up.

"I will be doing all the measurements and collecting the data. That data will then be given to your physician who will interpret it and go over the results with you."

ERGH! Basically, she was saying, "I'm not telling you a damn thing today!"

Notorious words we can all relate to when we have chest x-rays, MRIs, or even x-rays for a broken bone. That bone can be blatantly in two pieces in the picture and the x-ray technician will be like, "Okay, your doctor will be in touch with you in regard to the results."

Ugh!

The ultrasound was complete. True to her word, the technician did not say much regarding the measurements and data she accumulated. She did, however, comment on the babies' weights. She stated there was a significant difference in their weights. If I recall correctly, Twin A weighed around eight ounces, and Twin B was like twelve ounces.

It certainly did not register to Rick or me that this information was a sign of anything. We later found out it was a huge sign!

The hospital perinatologist came in as I was adjusting my shirt and getting up from the table. "Ruth, Rick, the results of the ultrasound show . . . "

Here come the definitive words. I prepared my mind and heart. I watched the perinatologist's lips move. I watched for his mouth to say, "Down syndrome."

But he said, "You have monoamniotic twins."

"What? What did you say?"

"Monoamniotic twins" he repeated.

"I'm sorry, what does that mean?"

Typically, twins develop each in their own sac. He explained that based on the ultrasound results the babies appeared to be in one sac. Thus, the word "mono," meaning "one."

"And what does this exactly mean?"

"It means your babies are at risk. This discovery officially makes you a complicated pregnancy."

WTF MAGGIE! There were those freaking words of wisdom again: "Twins come with twice the risk for complications."

The perinatologist continued to explain that since the babies are in one sac, their movements can cause their umbilical cords to become entangled. The biggest concern with this is strangulation or pinching off the cord to one or both babies.

Uh, what? I looked at Rick. His face looked as confused as mine was. We did not understand what this meant.

The doctor explained that early in the pregnancy, like now, the risks are lower as the babies are small and have plenty of room to move about in the sac. But as they grow, movement will become restricted. Restriction of movement can cause an umbilical cord or cords to get compressed or even wrapped around one of their necks.

Oh, lovely! This just sounds fricking lovely!

He continued to say as a complicated, high-risk pregnancy, I would require close monitoring with fetal kick testing, ultrasound monitoring, and growth monitoring.

WTF MAGGIE!

Dr. Maggie told me at my six or eight-week appointment that twins come with higher complications as if it was "a possibility," After receiving this news, I wondered why she just didn't tell me, "You are a complicated, high-risk pregnancy, period."

I do not like surprises, people! Do not throw me any surprise parties, do not try to surprise me with trips or gifts. Even expected presents make me uneasy. I do not like surprises, and I do not know how to react. I need time to process, prepare, and possibly fix.

Springing things on me causes me so much anxiety. These babies and their "surprises" were putting my mental health into a tizzy. Our beautiful baby boys were monoamniotic twins, and Down syndrome wasn't definitively ruled out.

***

My mom!

Her saying, "This isn't what I agreed to or signed up for" is funny to me. I whole-heartedly believe I did sign up for this!

Before I get started, I want to tell you something as you read on. These are my beliefs, my ways, my desires, my life, and my version to tell. As you read my perspective and my story, I am not asking you to agree, disagree, believe, not believe, or even understand my way of thinking. To each their own. I am merely sharing. What you take away from it is on you!

With that being said, do you believe in soul contracts? I do. I believe we are given a soul contract prior to being born. As a soul, an eternal being, I agreed to a particular contract. I agreed to come to Earth School. I knew Earth School would help me refine certain aspects of myself, to learn, teach, and grow.

As we learn and grow, we graduate from our spiritual levels. This allows each of us to not only expand but to help others. Your soul knows what it is doing. It is following through with a contract of what you will teach in Earth School as well as learn. This contract gives you the ability to navigate very challenging people, situations, relationships.

I can remember, even before I was born, that I wanted a challenge. I wanted something that would be worth living for. Something that would make every day different. I wanted something that would make me think and be able to handle crucial situations. I felt strongly that I could help others tremendously through my contract. I wanted to bring awareness.

16

I wanted to help reduce resistance in the world. People struggle to accept others and often judge harshly. This resistance leads to placing limits on individuals preventing them from reaching their full potential. It is import- ant to promote unconditional love and support instead of love that depends on certain conditions. By encouraging this acceptance and understanding I would be trying to create a more inclusive and compassionate community for everyone.

I picked my family. A family I knew would be strong and that I would be able to utilize to teach.

You see, you are reading my mom's story, and she is striking your emo- tions with the complications, the anguish, and the hardships. Her story highlights medical challenges, fear, overwhelmingness, emotional roller coasters, and uncertainty. She is dwelling on the outcomes. Things are not always what you plan for or expect, and she is resisting what is happening and only focusing on what she wants.

The spiritual meaning behind "surrender" is to stop struggling against what is. To surrender is to let go of the smallness of life and fully embrace its totality. Surrendering allows us to detach from the outcome. It helps us stop trying to control outcomes and encourages us to accept what is. If we believe all times are divinely guided and protected, then surrendering is easier to lean into. When you no longer resist and surrender to the flow of life, there is a peace and freedom that follows.

Suzanne Giesemann's spiritual guide says: "There is quite a difference between doing and being. With being, you flow. Picture a leaf in a stream. There is no effort. It is moving effortlessly with the current. In doing, there is effort. Oh, how much easier your life would be if you would learn to find that perfect sweet spot between doing and being, between effort and flowing. Yes, in human form you must take action; you must do. As a soul, you are at your best when you flow... just being the shine light- the natural expression of the One Light of Consciousness that you are. Do not go long periods of time simply doing. Alternate and integrate the two, and you will find your life flows in magical ways. You are so very loved."

The Universe is in motion. We get the opportunity to co-create our lives with the plans of the Universe. My mom was not co-creating yet; she was focusing on the outcome, trying to control the situation, and missing all the lessons.

Behind all the "mud" of the scary news—the uncertainty, the not understanding what any of this means—the love between my parents was growing stronger. My parents were learning things they would never have learned otherwise. They were unknowingly preparing for a life that would expand their souls, engorge their hearts, grow their compassion, enlarge their community, and make them stronger than they ever could have anticipated.

My mom said she didn't agree or sign up for this and that she doesn't like surprises. Little did she know, I did! I agreed to this story, this journey, this teaching, and I knew the lessons were for them. **Their devastation, shock, disbelief, and uncertainty was my happiness;** *happiness about being alive and being able to teach others while sharing my light.*

I Got This, Bro!

Being diagnosed with monoamniotic twins seemed vague to me. I didn't feel any different and wasn't worried as I felt like the babies would behave in the one sac and all would be well.

I was twenty-seven weeks pregnant, and it was Memorial Day weekend. I had been feeling movements on a regular basis, but I remember that weekend I was certain I distinguished two movements: like movement from Baby A and movement from Baby B! It was an incredible feeling that filled my heart with excitement and unconditional love for these two sweet babies.

On June 1, 1999, ten days shy from being seven months pregnant, I was scheduled for another ultrasound to measure growth and weight and monitor the one sac situation.

I thought, What a wonderful opportunity for my nieces, Athenia and Jenn, to witness an ultrasound with not just one, but two babies. As a medical professional, I always like to let others see, learn, experience, and enjoy the profoundness of healthcare and healing. If you recall, I had my husband, mom, mother-in-law, AND father-in-law in the delivery room when I delivered Leah. That was me, again, giving exposure to the miracle of life and hospital experience.

I don't remember why Rick wasn't at this ultrasound. But he wasn't. I think due to the multitude of appointments, testing, and ultrasounds, and his workload, we just thought it wasn't warranted. I'm not sure.

So, off to the hospital I went with my two nieces (Leah was in preschool) to do a "complicated pregnancy" ultrasound check-in. Shirt up, belly exposed, and gel squirted, the ultrasound began. It was only a hot minute before you could feel the tension in the room.

Nothing was said except, "The doctor will be in shortly."

Seconds, I honestly do not think it was even minutes later, the doctor walked in solemnly and broke the news.

"One of the babies, Baby B, has a halo effect, which means he has passed."

WHAT?? THIS CANNOT BE HAPPENING!

Anguish filled my soul. I couldn't believe what he said. I remember thinking This cannot be happening! I did not ask for twins. I was given twins so one could be taken away?

WTF Maggie times a million!

***

I don't remember the part of the soul contract that talked about losing my twin brother.

However, I do know that my brother, Jackson, is the one who guides me, gives me direction, strength, and oomph to continue this journey called life. I have always felt him and have had his voice in my head for as long as I remember. It is as though I carry his spirit within me.

I think the loss of my brother gave me the ability to be a stronger teacher, mentor, guide, and spiritual consultant. He and I shared utero, and in utero we shared conversations, plans, lessons, and ideas. It was not until later in life that I realized because of the loss of Jackson, or so I think, I was given the ability to be empathetic to others' feelings, to feel energies within a room, and to feel the presence from the other side.

"Halo Effect" is the term used to describe when a baby passes in utero. It is a white circle over the baby's head that is seen via ultrasound and looks like a halo. In my mind, this term is fitting, as Jackson would stay in angelic form, and I would enter in earthly form.

Physical bodies are merely vessels which carry our souls. My disabled body would be carrying two souls—mine and my identical brother's.

I got this, BRO!

Birth Right . . .
Be The Most You Can Be

I was admitted to the local hospital for observation. When a baby passes in utero, there are increased risks to the mom and existing baby. Risks that could include preterm labor, pre-eclampsia, and intrauterine growth restriction.

Our family came to visit Rick and I in the hospital to try and provide love and support. Depression had set in. I was not talking. I was not eating. I certainly was not entertaining guests.

After further testing and observation, it was determined I needed to be transferred to a hospital that provided level three prenatal care. At that hospital, it was determined my pregnancy was not of monoamniotic twins but twin-to-twin transfusion syndrome.

Twin-to-twin transfusion syndrome (TTTS) is where the babies play tug-of-war for nutrients, blood, and oxygen. It is a placental issue versus a baby issue. One vessel provides for both babies, and there becomes a donor twin and a recipient twin.

The misdiagnosis came from the fact that the recipient twin's pull was so extraordinary Baby B's sac was like plastic wrap around him and couldn't be seen. Once Baby B passed, the suction was released, and the second sac could be seen floating freely in utero.

Back in 1999, they were just starting to test procedures to treat TTTS. The procedure utilized a laser to seal off the vessel and disconnect them permanently. Today there is a perfect process and effective treatment for TTTS.

Following the explanation of the medical nightmare, the perinatologist at the level three hospital said, "I'm going to get you one healthy baby out of all this."

I won't go into further detail about the complications that continued throughout this pregnancy. Let's just say they were not pretty! They included depression (the thought of carrying a deceased baby and live baby consumed my soul), anger, pruritic urticarial papule, and plaques of pregnancy (PUPPP), and gestational diabetes, just to name a few.

To say I had reached my limit of "things" happening during this pregnancy would be an understatement. I didn't believe I was going to get a healthy baby after all the things I was going through. As a matter of fact, at every doctor visit I pleaded repeatedly to please just deliver these babies.

Prior to every visit, Rick would kindly ask me not to cuss at the doctor. It was just so emotional for me. It was a crying cussing fest! I remember yelling things like, "How would you like to be in your mom's belly with your dead brother?"

Rick's ultimate embarrassment was the visit when I could not take the itching from the PUPPP rash anymore. The doctor had prescribed steroids to treat the rash, which got me the diagnosis of gestational diabetes.

I cried—okay, I heavily sobbed, to Dr. Vogt that I could not live in an oatmeal bathtub, keep taking steroids that affected my blood sugar, or apply hydrocortisone cream ANY MORE!

He patiently and calmly said, "You are going to have to. We are almost there."

"I wish I could take some of this fucking rash and put it on your dick so you could understand my misery!" Not a proud moment in my life, but I was over it.

Rick was flabbergasted and by the look on his face I could tell he wanted to disappear.

Pfft! If anyone wanted to disappear, it was me!

The doctor remained professional and simply said, "Ruth, I understand how miserable this has been for you. We are so close. I will order a blood test to check for the lung maturity, and if it is sufficient, we will schedule your C-section.

Yes! Yes! I had been receiving injections to help with lung maturity so there was no way this baby's lungs were not mature at thirty-eight weeks!

The doctor was an expert and knew what he was talking about. I respected him; however, I was at the point where I didn't believe or trust anyone, especially in regard to this pregnancy.

As we sat on our back porch that evening watching hummingbirds at the feeder, the phone rang. It was the doctor. He explained the test results came back and showed the minimal result for lung maturity. He suggested we wait another week to deliver.

I was not having it. "You said if the blood work showed maturity, we would deliver. Low end, minimal end, it doesn't matter, it shows maturity!"

He went on to explain that if we delivered too early the baby could end up in neonatal intensive care to be monitored. He could require supplemental oxygen or even intubation, and have an extended hospital stay.

"Yeah, yeah. Doesn't matter—we are delivering. You said we could schedule delivery if the test was where it needs to be, and it is!"

On August 18, 1999, both the joy of life and the pain of death emerged. Later, in the recovery room holding Jackson Keith and reflecting on all the previous events, we realized that through

Jackson's death, Twin A had life. Although parting with Jackson was difficult, it gave us a ray of hope for our other son, Mason Grant. We resolved to see the glory in his survival.

We were so grateful for the doctor's knowledge, patience, and kindness. It was because of him we were holding Twin A, Mason Grant, the most beautiful baby boy in our arms.

***

My parents saw Jackson's passing as death. Sadness. Loss.

I never have had the feeling of sadness over Jackson. I only knew him in spiritual form, so I do not see it as a loss. I still have him with me like I did before I was born. He chose to stay in spirit form and work through me.

Little turd put a lot on me, wouldn't you say? But hey, he won fair and square. That tug of war in utero was a real thing. He pulled stronger and I lost my grip. He got the halo, and I was born.

***

At my six-week postpartum visit, I took the doctor and his staff a gift. Since it was near October, I gave them a cauldron full of all kinds of candy and snacks. Also, in the cauldron I put two boxes of Preparation H (hemorrhoid cream). In the card, I thanked them for all their care, kindness, and putting up with me. I explained the Preparation H was to be used for future patients who, like me, would be a pain in their ass!

***

That gift was epic! My parents should have kept one of the Preparation H creams for themselves. They didn't know they were the ones who were going to need it. My journey, as their son, would be nothing less than a pain in their asses.

Hahaha! This is going to be great! **Everyone's birth right is to be the most you can be.** *Since I was given the passage, I will do just that.*

Release the Emotion

Holy freaking moly Mason could cry. He would cry, and cry, and cry, and cry. We could not understand it.

The pediatrician declared "colic." We were prescribed specialized, expensive-ass formulas that were hypoallergenic or gentle. We used gas drops. We rocked, walked, drove, and bounced hours upon hours to try to get him to stop crying.

There was no relief. This child was miserable, and sorry to say, so were we! It was affecting our home. Lack of sleep, lack of peace, lack of being able to do anything due to Mason's discontentment. What baby doesn't fall asleep on a drive or in a swing?

HELP US!

On a Sunday, we went decided to go to the church we have attended for years. We dropped Leah off at Sunday School, then preceded to the nursery for Mason. We explained to the staff that Mason cries and there wasn't anything they could do except let him cry. They took the pumpkin seat that carried Mason and accepted him into their realm.

After the hour church service, we retrieved Leah and made our way to get Mason. When we entered the room, a staff member was holding a screaming Mason. She was distraught. Her words, I am sure, came out without thought: "I cannot watch him again. He has not quit crying since you left. This is not fair to the caregivers or the other children. I advise you to think about another way to attend the service."

Wowza!

I took Mason and didn't say a word to Rick or Leah until we got to the car. Then, with tears in my eyes, my voice shaking, I asked, "Did the church people just tell us our son is not welcome there? For crying out loud, I was only wanting an hour for myself. I was hoping that a church service could rejuvenate me, give me the spiritual guidance I needed to get through the week of his crying. One hour! I listen to him cry the other twenty-three hours of the day times seven days a week!"

Rick's gentle response: "I know honey, I know. I understand."

The next day I dropped Leah off at preschool and decided I needed to drive through an ATM to get some cash. Mason was being his normal, cute self (NOT!) in his car seat—screaming, screaming, and screaming. A blood-curdling, high-pitched shrieking cry that went through your soul. I could feel my nerves unraveling, my chest rising, and I was trying to breathe, in and out.

My inner voice was trying to calm me down, explaining, "He is just a baby; he can't help it." Then it switched to, "Something MUST be wrong. Maybe I am missing something? Maybe it's me? Maybe I'm not being a good mom?"

As my heart raced, my mind went from one thought to another, and the high shrills filled the interior of the car. I must have unknowingly released the brake, because I smacked right into the back of the car in front of me. I jerked the car into park, jumped out of the car, and tearily said, "I'm so sorry! I am so sorry!"

The irritation and disbelief on this person's face said it all! "What in the actual world, lady?"

In a panic, I tried to explain to the gentleman that I had a newborn in the car. He cries all the time. I have not gotten much sleep. I am so sorry. Blah, blah, blah. I was blubbering.

The driver looked at me like I was a psychopath. He looked at his car, shook his head, got into the driver's seat, and left.

I certainly didn't feel any empathy or caring about my circumstance. I got in the car, put my head in my hands, and cried right along with Mason. My cry was sobbing, hard, and nostril-breathing, whereas Mason's cry remained shrill. I called my husband. He encouraged me to make an appointment with the pediatrician to see if they could do anything else for Mason.

At the appointment, the pediatrician could tell I was exasperated, exhausted, and near my wits' end. Yet, she had the same demeanor as the driver of the car I bumped into at the ATM.

"Not sure what to do or tell you."

She suggested respite care with family and friends, and taking time for us. She assured me the baby was not in pain, and to let him cry was okay. She emphasized it was best to put the baby in his room and shut the door than to take my emotions out on him.

I knew what she was saying to me: DO NOT SHAKE THE BABY! I had no intention of ever shaking the baby, but I was about to shake her if she didn't help us!

The visit did not give me much to go on or any consolation. She suggested some remedy for gastric reflux and sent us on our way.

After a multitude of weeks, we found a solution! A short, sporadic solution, but it worked!

When we turned the vacuum on, Mason would stop crying. He would immediately stop, eyes wide open, and just stare and be content. So, we did what we had to do. We would turn the vacuum on, not to actually clean, just to quiet our little guy. We could leave the vacuum on for an hour and Mason would not make a peep, but as soon as it was turned off he would scream again.

Weird, but hey, we took what we could get.

Fortunately, we had supportive parents, and they gave us some respite. They would come to our house to watch Mason so we could get things done. Sometimes we would even take Mason to their home so Rick and I could go out to dinner or take Leah to a movie or something. Just to get some time away.

But let's be clear, Mason's grandparents could only do it for so long. After a couple of hours, they were done too! We understood, and we appreciated what they did and could offer.

Exhaustion.

Sadness.

Tears.

His cries made us all want to cry.

Day in and day out.

***

My non-stop crying as I saw it was twofold.

First, I was emotional. I had left the spiritual world, came out of my mother's womb, and just lost physical contact with my brother. I entered this unknown place where I knew I would ultimately teach, but didn't quite know what that would exactly look like. My eternal soul was having a human experience. A little overwhelming for an infant, wouldn't you say?

Second, due to my complicated birth, my neurological system was in overdrive! Every noise, movement, or task was overstimulating. I couldn't regulate anything. I couldn't calm my nerves. I couldn't process the things I was supposed to do. I did not want to eat. I did not know what to do. So, I cried and cried and cried. I couldn't stop crying.

As far as the vacuum—yes, I stopped crying when my parents turned it on. I was freaking paralyzed in fear! I laid as quiet as I could because I knew I was about to be murdered. LOL!

This paralyzing fear of the vacuum would follow me in life. I am glad my parents had some relief from my crying, but this relief was one of the first things that introduced me to being afraid!

The other side (spiritual side) is a place full of love. This side (physical side) is a world full of fear.

Fear of illness.

Fear of scarcity.

Fear of anything that is "different."

Fear of loss, not only of people, but even in simpler things, like sports or work.

Fear makes us put on masks. Fear causes anger, stress, depression. Fear lowers our energy. Fear limits our growth.

There are many who choose not to face their fears, and they fall prey to addictions or vices to escape them. These types of escape, along with the fear (because the vices don't take away or cure the fear), increase the struggle. There is a reason alcohol got the name liquid courage. It is not in anyone's best interest to hide, cover, or numb feelings. You see, these vices dim our abilities and our lights. They lower our energy frequency.

*It is important for us to feel the feels. By us feeling our emotions, and riding them out, we will learn from them. Addressing our emotions and fear, we become stronger, brighter, and of higher essence. **Inhale the uncomfortable feelings and release the emotion into the Universe.***

I'm Just Happy to Be Here

Mason had a misshaped head. It was football-shaped. He also continued to cry and was not meeting developmental milestones. So, at three months of age the pediatrician decided to order a CT scan and MRI during Mason's wellness check. This decision didn't bother me as I really didn't think much of it. I waited for the call from scheduling to get the test done. The call came, and the test was scheduled.

Since he was an infant and obviously would not be able to stay still for the procedure, he would require sedation. Because of the sedation he would have to stay overnight to be observed and watched.

Sounds like a plan. Let's do it.

I don't remember a whole lot about him having the test, but I do remember he was placed in the PICU (Pediatric Intensive Care Unit) at Children's Hospital after the test. It was because of a bed issue, not because of a critical status or concern.

I can still see Rick and I in the PICU with crib after crib lined up; a multitude of babies with parents cooing over their precious little ones. It was a surreal experience, because we knew most of the babies were in there because of complicated medical conditions.

We felt sad and sorry for them, and I remember talking about how hard it must be for them.

After Mason received the scan, a hospital pediatrician came in and told us the results of CT scan and MRI had been read.

We looked at him, and were like, "Okay?"

His presence felt off, a little awkward, but not much. He began with, "Mr. and Mrs. Bailey."

If a medical professional ever addresses you formally, there is value or importance in what they are going to say. So log that into your memory box.

"Mr. and Mrs. Bailey, your son's MRI showed periventricular leukomalacia, or PVL."

Rick and I looked at each other, and I said, "Okay?"

The pediatrician and I locked eyes. "That means we will have to monitor him closely, watch how he meets or doesn't meet milestones, and go from there."

I was still confused. "What should Rick and I be doing in regard to this?"

His exact words were, "Take the child home and love him."

I was perplexed. Uh, we were going to do that of course, but I mean, what kind of things did we need to do to help him reach milestones, to help him get over this?

He went on to tell us every child who has periventricular leukomalacia is different and they respond differently, regardless of having the same diagnosis.

I pushed. "Doctor, I need a little more information. I need to know what we are looking for, at, and what this means for him."

He said in his matter-of-fact way, "Ma'am, it means your son may never crawl, walk, or talk. He is likely to develop some form of cerebral palsy. You need to take him home, love him, and just wait and see."

My heart stopped.

WTF Maggie!

My next thought was the delivery doctor and his statement to us. You said you were going to get us a healthy baby out of this! Is this a healthy baby?

The pediatrician continued. "Please don't Google this diagnosis as you will only see the worst. Google is not a doctor and not an accurate resource to use." Off he went to see another patient.

Rick and I stood there starting at each other, speechless. Then our eyes went to our beautiful baby boy, Mason, laying so contently in the crib. What was that man even talking about? Our baby was perfect. Other than his misshaped head he was fine. Most babies are born with a cone-shaped head due to coming out of the vaginal canal or the use of forceps. But Mason was delivered via C-section, and his misshaped head was horizontal, not vertical. To me, it was the same but different, lol.

Being the planner, preparer, and surprise-hater I am, what do you think I did immediately?

Yup! Got on Google.

Oddly, it was very unspecific. It defined PVL as the softening of the white matter around the ventricles. I did not understand the significance of PVL. And honestly, we had heard so many things from medical professionals in the past year or so that ended up not being accurate or true, I was not trusting anything anyone said anymore. Maybe I was becoming a "the data don't add up" type of girl, like Rick. I don't know.

***

Let's talk about diagnoses.

Down syndrome. Monoamniotic twins, TTTS, PVL, colic, PUPPP, gestational diabetes, cerebral palsy—the list goes on and on.

Look at how the diagnosis given at the time put my parents into a spin. Look how the diagnosis started to manage my mom's thoughts and feelings.

From a diagnosis, my mom began thinking about prognosis, treatment, deficits, fixing, overcoming, and adapting.

Hunh!

Labels.

Once a person is given a label, the view of the person changes. People put their own opinions and thoughts into what that label means. When you are labeled due to a diagnosis, or certain beliefs, or a certain lifestyle (rich, poor, gay, or straight), or skin tones, or cultures, you must battle for your life to be as meaningful, because this world has a hard time accepting differences. Labels can promote hate, disgust, loathing, and most importantly, division.

I've never really understood it.

People. We are all just people. People who seek love, acceptance, opportunity, equality—yet a label immediately dissolves that.

Take a minute and think about that. If someone doesn't act or think like you, do you accept it, or do you try to convince them to think like you? Does your view of them change due to the label? I have had so many experiences where everyone wants me to be who they think I should be and do what they think I should do.

It has been exhausting!

There are so many people who struggle living this life, and this is a big reason why. Labels and judgment.

Remember me talking about the baby crying as they come into the world? A baby, pure, divine love, born authentically themselves will spend a lifetime trying to conform to its parents' beliefs, societal norms, culture expectations, and definitions of success. Their being and existence will begin to transform. As they transform, whether or not through good intentions, they will lose their identity, their self. They will start to be programmed to try and feel love, acceptance, belonging and worth through others' eyes.

However, the biggest and most important thing any person can do is to love themselves and be authentic! The world hasn't allowed this yet. On the other side, there is no division. There are no diagnoses or labels. There is no hate. Only unconditional love.

It may sound cheesy, but it is the truth.

Heaven doesn't have pockets of groups. Monetary wealth on Earth doesn't make your entrance gates any pearlier. Who you loved or the color of your skin is not judged in heaven. The amount of people you brought to church with you is not recorded. All those things are left here on Earth.

I must laugh because right now I am probably being judged and labeled because someone reading this doesn't agree with what I am writing. I'm fine with that.

Just please, consider . . .

Stop fighting.

Stop judging.

Stop hating.

Stop dividing.

We are all human. Human, kind—be both!

***

I really wish my mom would have been able to not worry about the medical stuff. All that precious time she spent did no one any good, especially her. She received the ultimate message from the doctor: "Take him home and love him." But to her, loving meant "How can I fix him?" "How can I help my precious child?" "What do I need to do?"

Don't get me wrong, I get it! She wanted the best for me. My mom and dad love me tremendously. Ultimately, she was scared for me. She knew that if I didn't crawl, walk, talk, etc., the world was not going to be kind to me. She knew physical limitations would cause challenges and exclude me. She wasn't necessarily fighting for me, but more for others to accept me and be kind to me. She knew that she, my dad, Leah, and the strong family circle would take care of me, love me, and give me the best. She was worried about those outside our ring.

Pfft!

I was just happy to be here.

Time for Me to Shake Things Up

We took Mason home from the PICU and continued the journey as a family.

Adjusting to being a family of four was challenging. My pregnancy with the twins was anything but normal. The multitude of appointments to figure things out, monitor things, and keep everyone healthy was overwhelming and time-consuming.

Due to this, "mommy time" was taken away from Leah. Playdates with friends and other moms no longer included me. I felt the stress, tension, worry, and apprehension to my core. I tried very hard not to let it impact Leah and her care, but it was difficult! We were blessed with family and friends who jumped in to help care for, entertain, love, and keep Leah busy during that difficult time.

Months after delivery, we were mourning the loss of our precious Jackson and dealing with a newborn who would not stop crying. Learning of Mason's brain injury because of the pregnancy made it seem like things were not going to be looking up. It was more a huge slap-in-the-face reality check. This scenario was not one I planned for or envisioned when Rick and I started discussing becoming a family of four.

You know that six-to-twelve-week period in the Family Medical Leave Act (FMLA) that allows you to have time off to bond with your new baby? There wasn't much bonding going on between me and Mason or Leah. It was survival mode. I had to make sure everyone was clean, fed, and safe. If I did those things, it was a good day.

This new family unit we were becoming was one of exhaustion beyond the typical caring for a three-year-old and newborn exhaustion. The physical and mental toll was crushing me. By the time, Rick came home for work, I was either in tears or on the verge of tears.

Mason's infancy had all of us waiting and watching for him to meet developmental milestones, and it wasn't happening. Mason was not able to sit up by himself without being supported. When he was laid on the floor, his arms were stiff behind him, his legs straight; he looked like a fish out of water! At the eight-month mark, if we got his arms out in front of him, he would army crawl, dragging his straight legs behind him.

***

My mom was in a state of stress, apprehension, and tension. She was full of worry. She was searching for hope and happiness through me being able to sit up or crawl. Her energy was dwindling, physical and mental. She was right that she was in survival mode.

But what good is that for her, Leah, or me?

Second to second, breath to breath, moment to moment. Life is a string of moments. Each moment holds a place. It is so important to take them in. Most people don't stop, breathe, look, listen, and relate very often. They don't take in the sunshine, feel the grass between their toes, or stop to see the beauty and growth around them.

No matter the circumstance, there is a blessing in the moment.

If there is one thought I can give you, let it be this: open your mind and expand your heart to all the moments around you. Hope and happiness are not in obtaining skills or things, meeting goals, or developing success; hope and happiness comes from within us.

Not to sound harsh, but everyone in the Bailey home was living with blinders on. You know, the quaint neighborhood, white picket fence, cute family, and smooth sailing type of blinders. They were only able to see and compare what was happening to what they were dreaming of.

*But we can't control all things. The Universe is at play. There are lessons to be learned, people to meet, things to change, challenges to overcome. All these things could not be done living in Mayberry. **It was time to shake things up!***

Who better to do that than good ole me?

Angels Among Us

At the age of one, Mason was given the official diagnosis of cerebral palsy. They said they needed to monitor the child and see what milestones were reached and not reached for one year before they would diagnose. Mason 100% was not meeting milestones and the scan had indicated the brain injury.

Our infant was diagnosed with cerebral palsy!

Definition: Cerebral palsy (CP) is a group of neurological disorders that affect a person's ability to control their muscles and movement. It's caused by damage to the developing brain or abnormal brain development that occurs before or during birth (congenital CP) or during the first years of a child's life (acquired CP). CP is the most common motor disability in childhood and can affect nervous system functions like learning, hearing, seeing, and thinking.

Brain damage.

Our baby had brain damage, which wouldn't allow his body to move the way it should. It was possible our baby would never crawl, walk, or talk.

Momma Bear mode ON! I would be doing anything and everything to give my precious child the opportunity to do those things and more. I was not going to allow a scan and diagnosis to determine my child's future.

Leah's preschool years continued to be years of going with Mommy and Mason to:

- Doctors' appointments, including primary care, neurology, physical medicine and rehab (PMR), orthopedic and development, and behavior pediatrician (DBP)
- Evaluations
- Assessments
- Physical therapy
- Occupational therapy
- Durable medical equipment appointments
- Early intervention programs

And when we weren't going somewhere to see someone, they were coming to our home, or we were filling out needed paperwork or on the phone with one of the following:

- County workers
- Early intervention home teachers
- Bureau for Children with Medical Handicaps (BCMH)
- Service waitlists
- Insurance companies

I was overwhelmed by the amount of information being thrown at me. The rules. The regulations. The succession of things—you must do this before he can get that. You must complete this before that is covered. He must be able to do this before we can look at that.

Without intention, Leah was being molded into a stronger "mommy's helper" by helping with Mason. She saw the need. She felt the tension. Playtime with her brother wasn't just playtime—it was therapy. I would catch her stretching Mason's legs, encouraging him to reach for the toy, or just entertaining him to take the pressure off me.

Now that Mason had an official diagnosis, our county was able to provide us with early intervention services. These services included sending out an early interventionist to our home. Our early interventionist was Ms. Martha.

Ms. Martha came and did evaluations and assessments on Mason. She would work with Mason on skills such as sitting up and holding a ball or spoon, encourage verbal output, and was such an incredible support to us as a family. She was the very first ray of sunshine and hope we encountered after having Mason. She was so positive, so encouraging, extremely knowledgeable, and was able to provide us information on what to look for and how to do things. She provided resources for certain toys, equipment, and classes such as music therapy and infant massage.

Ms. Martha came to our home each week, and to say we waited at the door for her is not an overstatement. Meeting and working with her was the first time we didn't feel isolated or like things were unmanageable. She was a breath of fresh air!

Ms. Martha continued to work with Mason at home until he was two years old. Once, he turned two he was eligible for an early intervention preschool program. Ms. Martha was his teacher in this program, along with an assistant teacher, Ms. Carol. The classroom had six to eight students, and a parent would attend with their child.

In this classroom, Ms. Martha and Ms. Carol embraced each student and parent and helped them reach for the stars. We played in shaving cream, scooped pumpkins, learned the alphabet, sang songs, played instruments, and enjoyed a camaraderie with each other. It was in this classroom that the isolation of being the only mom or family dealing with a child who had special needs was diminished. Here were other children and parents in the same boat wanting the best for their child, just like us!

We were part of the "special needs club." It is a club that no one asks or wants to join, but once initiated you are immediately accepted, understood, and among your own. There are not strong enough words for the impact these fellow club members had on me and my soul. I have true gratitude towards Kelly's dad, Ron, Ethan's mom, Pam, Nolan's mom, Shannon, and so many others.

It was in this classroom that Mason met his first best friend, Nolan. Nolan had the biggest bluest eyes and purest white blond hair I had ever seen. He was as handsome as he was spunky! Nolan was challenged with gross motor delays, seizures, and speech deficits. But it didn't matter. Mason saw Nolan as someone to play with, someone who he enjoyed being around, and someone to have fun with. Nolan did not see or care about Mason's walker; he saw the same things Mason did—someone to play and have fun with.

As Nolan and Mason's friendship developed so did his mom's and mine. Shannon and I took the boys to each other's houses for playdates. We took trips to the park, museum, or pool. Together, we felt strong. We supported each other, helped each other. She would help me finagle Mason's walker, stroller, and diaper bag. I would help her decipher Nolan's desires as the words weren't always there. These special times in Mason's and my life are etched into my core.

Mason and Nolan remained friends for a couple of years until Nolan's dad accepted his medical residency in Wisconsin and the family had to move there. The separation was hard for Mason, and for me! We still to this day look at pictures of him and Nolan in Early Intervention classes together and reminisce on those special times shared.

Other playdates with Leah's preschool friends and their siblings were difficult. We could be at a park, and the kids would be running or going down the slide. By the time, I got Mason up the ladder of the slide, and in my lap to slide down, the other children and fellow moms were pushing each other on the swings on the other side of the playground.

I felt guilty that Leah's friends' parents had to watch her for me, not that she was hard to watch. I felt guilty that I couldn't push her on the swing or be part of the group hide-and-seek game. I would sit on the hillside with Mason and entertain him in his stroller with musical toys and watch all the families and children enjoy "typical" playground time.

It was not easy. Hard, actually. Very hard.

Our home had a large, enclosed porch overlooking the back-yard. This porch was a place that Leah, Mason, and I spent many summer afternoons playing together. We would do crafts, listen to music, and read books. It was sort of my safe place with the two kids. Mason was close by, safe, and Leah was contained as well as entertained. I'm not going to lie though; I housed inner sadness and loneliness as I heard the neighbor children playing tag, saw a group of children digging in the sandbox a door over, watched the boys two doors down play football, heard the laughter and glee from the neighborhood as their parents gathered together and talked, while my children and I were contained in a porch.

Our home also had an inground pool, so as much as possible, I would invite neighbors over to swim. This was a manageable activity, and swimming was also good therapy for Mason and his muscles. Between swim lessons, inflatable swim devices, and other children and parents present, it felt like the safety bases were well covered. It was fun for all, and everyone was included.

However, our pool gave me a scare when Mason was young. Leah had been invited to a friend's house, so Mason and I were home alone. I decided to sit poolside with Mason on the steps in the shallow end. It was a hot, humid day. Mason was wedged in the corner with me right next to him. We had our bathing suits on and were enjoying having our legs in the water. In a fraction of a second, Mason stiffened up his legs, which caused his body to slide off the step into the water. I was right there, but as quick as it happened it felt like eternity. I will never forget seeing him underwater with eyes wide open and the fear in his face. Again, I was right there, but reaching down for him felt like slow motion in a movie. They say life can change in an instant, and it's true. As I pulled him up, he sputtered and spit. I exhaled and started breathing again. I frantically scooped him up, firmly patted his back, and kept repeating "thank you, thank you, thank you." That was the last time we were in or near the pool by ourselves.

Leah's preschool was hosted at our community church.

One day, when I dropped Leah off at preschool, I noticed the church was having a vendor fair. So, after walking her into her classroom, I went down to the main area, carrying Mason on my hip. There were tables set up with books, Tupperware, make-up, and crafts. I came across a jewelry table and wanted to try on the bracelets displayed, but I had to put Mason down to do so. I sat him on the floor, right next to me. Now, when I say sat, it was really stabilized, because Mason could not sit up by himself. With the tightness and spasticity of his legs, if you tried to sit him up, he merely tumbled over.

A "sit" that is well-known to special needs children is the "W sit." It looks like a W with their legs bent back and wide. Sitting this way stabilizes the child; however, medically this type of sit is not recommended due to the strain on the hips and knees especially as the child gets older.

As Mason was sitting next to me, and I was fumbling with a bracelet, a lady who was selling books at the table behind us came over to me.

She said, "I think our children may have something in common."

My initial thought was, "I doubt it," but let her continue.

She went onto explain how she saw me stabilizing Mason and that her daughter requires the same type of sit pattern to stay upright.

WHAT?! I thought. I responded with, "Oh really?" I continued, "Well, Mason has spastic diplegia cerebral palsy which affects his legs." I waited for the "I'm sorry" look and uncomfortable silence that usually follows when people don't know what to say or do after that.

"My daughter, Mary, does too!"

It turned out that she and her husband had adopted a child from India who was near the same age as Mason.

Special needs club member!

Immediate bonding.

Immediate understanding.

Immediate acceptance.

Immediate friendship.

It is weird and hard to explain, but members of the special needs club know exactly what I am referring to. This introduction brought a new friendship to Mason and me. A friendship that would share in similarities, triumphs, challenges, and hurdles.

At the age of three, Mason was eligible for preschool within the school district. The district preschool setting was inclusive, meaning each classroom was integrated with typical students as well as students with educational challenges.

It was a unique setting as it was a large, open classroom. In each of the four corners of the classroom, there was a "class" with its own students, teacher, and assistant teacher. At the time, I wasn't sure how this setup was going to work, but it did. It actually worked well. The school district had impeccable teachers, and physical, occupational, and speech therapists, and were well-versed in managing an inclusive environment.

Several weeks into the preschool year, it became apparent that Mason had an extreme fear of the custodians. Anytime he could see a custodian, whether down the hall or in the classroom, he would freeze. His attention to task would be non-existent, and he would be hyper-focused on the custodian. His teacher could not understand it. When she brought it to my attention, I didn't have a clue either.

After this fear went on for a few months, his teacher thought maybe having the custodians come into the classroom and introduce themselves to the students may help. At this introduction, the students were able to ask questions.

Mason's hand shot up. "Do you have vacuum sweepers?"

"Well yes, we do."

"Can you not use them when we are in the classroom?"

The custodians exchanged looks with his teacher and responded, "We can certainly try not to, young man."

After that, Mason's fear of the custodians wasn't as extreme, although still present.

I remember one morning trying to get Mason into the classroom. I had him, his reverse Kaye walker, book bag, and my keys. The physical therapist, Ms. Simon, came out to the car to try and help me, but I was already loaded up and didn't see how I could transfer things over to her without disrupting what I had settled. While I appreciated her offer to help, I felt like it was a little too late at this point.

Ms. Simon was a petite, small-boned, thin woman. She exclaimed, "I have no idea how you are managing and carrying all of that!"

I laughed and said, "It's called Pack Mule!"

Ms. Simon continued, "You must take care of yourself. You certainly do not want to pull your back out or strain something."

I knew she had a point, but at the time I discounted it. I was merely trying to do what I could do and meet the needs of everyone, especially my son challenged by CP. Years later, I continue to hear that statement louder and clearer, and it resonates stronger.

My back has been affected by a high school sled riding injury, a nursing career, and Mason. I have pulled my back out on more than one occasion. I have been laid up and incapacitated where I have not been able to help my family.

As mothers, we work hard. We work super hard to meet the needs of our family and especially our children. When our children struggle, we work even harder to help them. Unfortunately, this can be at our own expense.

***

After several months, we had transitioned Mason to taking the bus to preschool. Fortunately, our driveway ended at a main street and the bus was able to pick him up there. One morning, as we were waiting for Mason's bus to take him to preschool, a lady pulled her car over on the berm of our yard and got out.

She said, "Good morning! Would it be okay if I prayed over your little boy?"

It felt strange, but I said "Sure."

With that she went over and laid her hands on top of Mason's head as he stood in his reverse Kaye walker and she prayed. I don't recall her words, or even if she prayed out loud. But I remember the incident. As quick as she came, she was gone.

Mason wheeled his walker over to me with his legs struggling behind and asked "Mom, what was that all about?"

I simply said, "I believe she was praying for healing on your behalf."

Without missing a beat Mason said, "Okay, but does that lady realize I don't need to be healed?"

Mason never saw anything wrong with himself.

***

The last thing I ever wanted to do was to cause my parents tension, stress, or pain. And I certainly did not mean to take away my sister's childhood and make her become a caregiver at the age of three.

I was just living life day by day, my friends.

When you think of angels you may think of ecclesiastic beings who have white wings and white dresses and float around. Have you ever thought that there are angels placed on this Earth to walk alongside us, not float above? Angels are here to guide, protect, and support us on our journey.

As a family, we have encountered SO many angels. They have shown up when we least expected them and helped us through the challenges we have encountered due to my cerebral palsy. These angels are everyday people. People who I don't even know if they recognize their extraordinary impact on our lives to this day, or the fact they are seen as earthly angels. I recognized them and knew them at first sight!

Let's begin with Ms. Martha. She walked through the doors of our home illuminating love, acceptance, and a "we got this" attitude. She didn't demonstrate one ounce of fear or uncertainty, only love. She grabbed me up without hesitation, talked, hugged, and shared moments with my mom and me from day one. We all became friends and even family in a short amount of time.

Ms. Carol was the assistant teacher with Ms. Martha at my preschool. She, too, emitted a glow of light. She was friendly, kind, accepting, and placed on this Earth to do the Divine's work. She knew it. She enjoyed it. As with Ms. Martha, she also spread love day to day to each and every student.

Special needs, disability, or challenging behaviors did not scare Ms. Carol.

My friends, Nolan, Ethan, Kelly, Mary, and so many others I have and have had are kindred spirits. We are all here to do spiritual undertakings. The Divine is working with us and through us for greater good.

Mary was born in India. A perfect example of how spirits far and near can come together to impact the world.

A MUDDY LIFE

My dear friend, Nolan. He and I saw each other for each other—we didn't see any physical disabilities; we didn't see any limitations. We laughed, played, enjoyed, and both knew instantaneously that this is how life (physically and spiritually) was meant to be. No limitations. We understood each other and our purpose here. I treasure the memories of my first true friend here on Earth.

Nolan left his physical body after they moved to Wisconsin when he was merely ten years old after a traumatic seizure. Nolan was an advanced soul. In his ten short years, his birth was what made his parents become parents. He embraced wordless communication without hesitation because he was comfortable with it from the other side. He showed us words are not needed to understand, love, or grow. He instilled love, patience, compassion, empathy, care, and kindness to those around him. He gave many different lenses to look through to those who didn't realize their sight was oblique. His impact continues through his family and his spirit prevails. I absolutely loved that guy!

The bonding of "club member" parents helps make changes in the world. They will strengthen each other and provide powerful improvements to the community for children with special needs. The things accomplished will be things that could not be accomplished just by one person.

***

I told you the vacuum cleaner scare would follow me through life! Those custodians with their damn vacuum cleaners, lawn mowers, and loud machines! Petrified me every day. No one came at me with a vacuum cleaner, but the enormity of the sound was enough for me to be quiet as an infant, and as a preschooler.

***

When that lady stopped to pray for me, I was more worried about her being a stranger than I was about anything she was doing or saying. I was baffled why my mom would let a stranger get out of her car and touch me! The lady was nice. She prayed over me and provided me with more strength to live out my purpose. She or my mom may have thought it was for my healing, but it wasn't. Of course there are miracles, and of course there can be healing, but I came here solid in my work to teach, grow, and expand, and I knew those things could not be achieved if I was healed from my cerebral palsy. That led to me saying, "Does she realize I don't need to be healed?"

Regardless, all examples mentioned above are just angels among us.

Nothing is By Coincidence

Rick has always been a hands-on, involved dad. He has never let Mason's diagnosis slow him down from being the dad he needs to be.

The only time I have seen life put Rick into a standstill was the loss of Jackson. During that time, Rick was quiet, standoffish, and just sad. His depression and loss were palpable. He was grieving. I was grieving. We had to grieve in our own ways, individually, and together. The grief, along with the Mason's diagnosis, shrill screaming, and raising a four-year-old daughter, was incredibly trying for us as a couple and as a family.

***

One evening, when Mason was about two, Rick decided to take Mason and Dory, our dachshund mix, on a trip to Target for something we needed at home. Rick parked the car in a handicap parking spot. He grabbed a cart that was nearby. He then reached in to unlatch Mason from his car seat, and that is when Dory jumped out of the car and took off in a mad dash.

When I say mad dash, I mean mad dash. Luckily, there was a huge grass lot on the side of the Target store. Dory took it upon herself to run laps, circles, and dashes in this field. Rick quickly got Mason into the cart, which was quite the process between maneuvering his stiff legs and getting him propped up.

"Dory! Dory! Come Dory!" Rick yelled as he pushed the cart toward the field near the store. And like an episode out of a comedic movie, Dory stopped, looked up at Rick and decided to run her happy little self in the other direction.

Rick knew right away what was going to happen. As the electronic doors opened for customers who were going in, Dory shot straight through the doors and into the store, full speed ahead.

Rick remembers saying "NOOOOOOOOOOOOO!" in his head. He rushed toward the store. She was gone, nowhere to be seen.

Rick, seriously questioning his life at this point, thought, WTF Dory!

He slowly went through the automated doors and into the store. He was met by an employee who had Dory in a cart. He approached Rick and asked, "Is this your dog, sir?"

"Uh . . . yes. Yes, that is my dog."

He quickly put Dory into his cart and hightailed back to the car. Dog and Mason secured, he journeyed back home—without whatever he went to Target for.

***

Mason was approaching the age of three, and the spasticity in his legs was strong! Things were becoming increasingly difficult for us and him.

One afternoon at Frisch's, we maneuvered Mason into a highchair. Rick held him up as I bent his legs and put them in the holes of the highchair. Then, he had to be propped up with coats on either side so he wouldn't lean. It was a nice lunch, until it was time to leave. It took three of us to get Mason out of the highchair! Rick had to pick him up, I had to bend his legs, and my mom had to pull on the highchair. It was quite dramatic and embarrassingly scary for us!

Shortly after these two incidents, I came across an article about twins with spastic diplegia that underwent a procedure called selective dorsal rhizotomy (SDR). In an SDR, doctors tested nerve roots, then they would cut certain ones to decrease the spasticity. The article was about a well-known surgeon who was an expert in this field. He had handled thousands of cases and done tons of research. He was in Missouri, just six hours from our home.

As you have read our story you may have noticed the medical team has not always gotten things right. My pregnancy had an array of miscalculations. Mason's infancy was full of inconsistent diagnoses. I was always trying to stay ahead of the game with treatment options, opportunities, or possibilities. I did not want to have to experience wrong information or be a trial for the medical team- I wanted experts. Experts who were confident in their plan. This article conveyed a confident, strong, trail-blazing, compassionate, bad-ass surgeon.

With excitement, I shared the article with Mason's medical team, which included his pediatrician, physical rehabilitation doctor, and physical and occupational therapists. All of them were reluctant to give their blessing to considering or investigating such a procedure; however, they told us it was ultimately our decision.

Rick and I decided to make an appointment with the surgeon in Missouri. He did the most thorough exam Mason had ever had. He explained the procedure, recovery, and healing process. He told us even with this procedure Mason would still have some spasticity and would need a cane to walk. He stated he could see Mason doing some independent walking, like in a home where he could regain his balance using a wall or sturdy piece of furniture.

Because the procedure wasn't being offered locally, it wasn't covered by our insurance plan initially. However, after accumulating medical documentation of Mason's spasticity limiting his functional ability and proving this spasticity would cause future orthopedic surgeries, we were able to get our insurance company to approve the out-of-state procedure.

We were so thankful!

***

I was only a toddler when Dory escaped the car, but I can tell you that it was hysterical! Run Dory! Run! Pick me up some peanut butter and jelly while you're in Target, please.

I feel like my mom is trying to pin the situation on me, but I had nothing to do with that escape. I may have made it a little harder to go capture her, but I didn't cause it. I am not taking the rap for that one!

***

That magazine article my mom came across about SDR was the beginning of using my life and situation as a teaching tool. It was meant for her to read. It was the link not only to a surgery that improved my function, it was also necessary for me to fulfill my purpose. It led us to a medical team that would help us throughout my life.

My mom shared that article with her fellow families. That article sparked other families to pursue this option for their children. A strong group of families was uniting and was going to use its force to make change, improve the system, and help children who had spastic diplegia cerebral palsy in their area.

Nothing happens by coincidence, my friends.

Doing What I Was Meant to Do Here

If Mason underwent an SDR, he would require an immense amount of physical therapy. It was two-fold, as Mason's brain would trigger nerves that were no longer connected, and the nerve roots left intact would be triggering weak muscles. It was going to be a long road of physical therapy to re-train neurologically as well as physically to get Mason functional.

Our insurance company only allowed twenty physical therapy visits per calendar year. Daily therapy five days a week with the allotted amount only gave Mason one month of therapy. Not nearly enough to gain the strength and function he was going to need.

Back to it again.

We tried diligently to get the insurance to cover more physical therapy visits for Mason following such an intricate procedure. We tried to show the long-term financial savings for them, like we did when we asked for the procedure to be approved. We had our physician do a physician-to-physician appeal.

They were not budging.

Self-paid therapy visits cost hundreds of dollars. We couldn't afford that. At the same time, we couldn't give up on providing Mason a fighting chance to become as independent as he could.

As word traveled, family, friends, co-workers, and neighbors rallied around us. Fundraisers were planned left and right.

Talk about creativity!

There was a spaghetti dinner fundraiser, a neighborhood yard sale, a potluck dinner, a wacky wedding, a chili cook-off, a donation opportunity at Christmas, a football rally, a silent auction, a raffle and more!

Thousands of dollars were raised for the Mason Bailey Physical Therapy fund. So many people believed in us, in Mason and his abilities, and the hope for his future.

Our hearts were full.

* * *

I am merely a three-year-old boy at this time. Word was traveling that I was going to have a complicated spinal surgery that would require long-term intense therapy and my family needed help with the costs. My blonde-haired, blue-eyed picture of me in my walker was displayed at banks, libraries, and peoples' workplaces with a donation jar. Event after event was being planned and carried out.

All these things happening were promoting love, hope, and awareness. People were learning about cerebral palsy, what it was, and how it affected people. People were focusing on helping me and my family, not on themselves or their own problems. People were coming together to provide love, support, and camaraderie. As I attended these events, my heart was so full, and it wasn't because of the money being raised but the unconditional love being shared not only for me and my family but for everyone in attendance. People were hugging, laughing, eating, playing, and enjoying each other's company. They were in the moment.

Yes! Yes! ***I was doing what I meant to do here!***

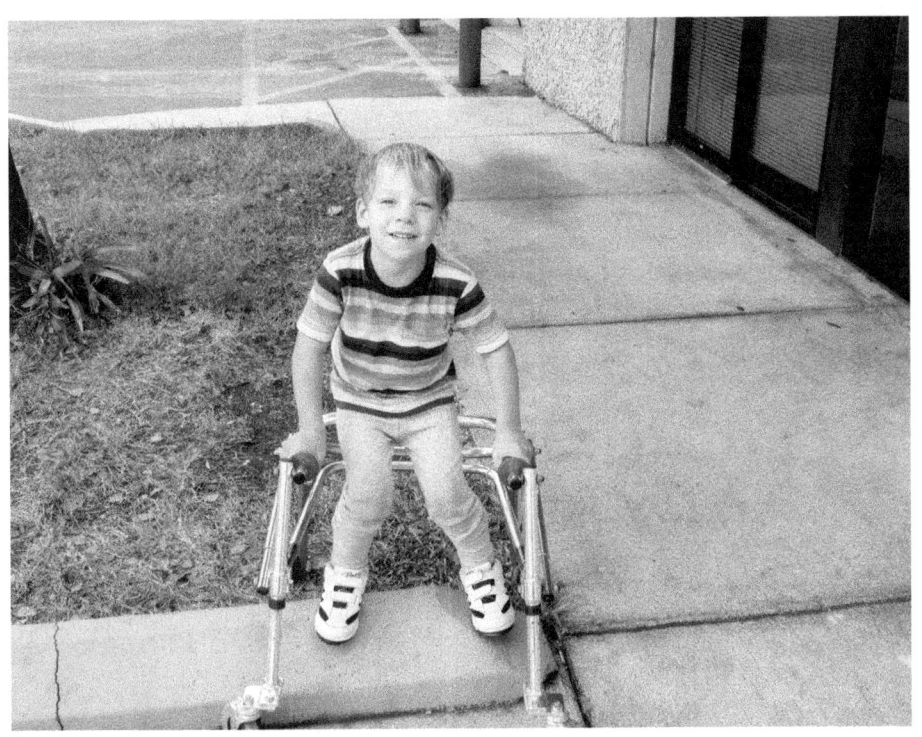

Superman

Looking back to when I didn't know what I know now, there was a lot of hope and optimism that the SDR surgery could make Mason an independent walker. This was something everyone was on board with and wanted for him.

It was during this time of planning for this huge surgery that Mason's current physical therapist mentioned the possibility of getting him a wheelchair. This suggestion made us feel she was giving up on Mason walking, and we worried it would provide him an easier way to get around, thus he would not work as hard. Rick and I were not having it!

The therapist explained many parents think that, but that isn't the case. She said having a wheelchair and being able to use it themselves gives the kids independence. It's like a toddler who begins to walk and starts exploring and getting into things. A child who has not been mobile who is given a wheelchair and taught how to use it begins to explore and get into things.

So, we conceded to the wheelchair.

One weekend, we decided as a family to go on an outing to a museum. It was still chilly outside, and it was somewhere we hadn't been to before. The trip would require Mason to have his wheelchair, which we were still getting used to. However, Mason was good at rotating the wheels and maneuvering himself.

It was a Saturday, and the museum had quite a few visitors making their way through the displays. We would push Mason into various rooms, then allow him to explore around the room by himself. Things were going well, and we all were enjoying ourselves, until . . . out of the corner of my eye, I saw a ramp going down.

And where was Mason?

At the top of it!

Before I could say or do anything, he was off, going down the ramp alone.

I know you're thinking, "So?"

So, Mason had not been using his wheelchair for long and was not the best at slowing or stopping himself!

Off he went, full speed ahead, as I yelled, "Rick!"

Rick and I rushed over to the ramp in time to witness Mason abruptly stopping at the bottom of the ramp, causing himself to fly out of the chair and hit a gentleman in the ankles. It was one of those moments where the decision was hard. Do I rush to the scene and make sure everyone is okay? Or do we act like we never saw what happened and be as surprised as everyone else?

Honestly, my immediate reaction was neither of those. It was pure embarrassment combined with not wanting to claim the situation or the kid! Hahahahaha!

I still remember the man's reaction. Big eyes, astonishment at the situation mixed with sheer fear. He was stunned to see a "handicapped child" sprawled out on the floor. He bent down to see if Mason was okay, then looked around to see where his parents were.

Mason's laughter was loud and obnoxious; he was experiencing sheer joy at what had just happened. He thought it was the greatest, funniest, coolest thing he had ever done!

WTH Mason!

His wheelchair laying on its side; Mister Museum-goer beside himself; Mason laying on a dirty carpet that surely had given him rug burn on his knees, stomach, and arms.

Not funny!

After the man realized Mason was okay and parents were on the scene, we all joined forces to lift our stuntman back into his chair.

We saw the gentleman several times throughout the rest of our museum visit, and each time he would say, "Hey Superman!"

TOTAL EMBARRASSMENT!

***

Every time I remember the incident at the museum, I still giggle. It. Was. Epic!

You would have thought that gentleman was in a haunted house and had just seen an otherworldly creature. Man, did I think I was going to be in trouble! I remember after everyone regained composure, I felt so proud and accomplished. There was not an ounce of embarrassment in my body.

I had gone so fast! I had flown so high! I hoped everyone had seen my performance! It was incredible. I mean, I know, I could have hurt the guy by taking him out, but I was still ready to do it again.

***Superman!** He called me Superman! That was awesome!*

I Wanted to Go Home

I will never forget the night before Mason's SDR surgery. Rick and I were explaining to him about the surgery and how the surgeon was going to "fix his legs."

Mason responded, "But, there isn't anything wrong with my legs. Look at them. They're perfect!"

That hit our hearts!

The next morning as we wheeled Mason in his chair from the hotel to the hospital for surgery, a street sweeper came up the side of the street near us. Mason screamed! He was so scared; he thought for sure he was going to get murdered. Crying, yelling, screaming—he was inconsolable. We got him away from the area as fast as we could and into the quiet space of the building. There we spent time comforting him and explaining the machine was cleaning the streets, that it was just doing its job, and that it was not going to hurt him.

Surgery lasted several hours and went extremely well. Mason was transferred from the recovery room to the intensive care unit. That was where we got to see him for the first time.

Heart-wrenching. His little three-year-old body buried under sheets and blankets in a big bed. He was extremely pale. He had an IV with all kinds of medicines dripping into him and an oxygen mask on his small face.

I brushed his beautiful blonde hair back from his face, and his eyes fluttered.

"Mason honey, Mommy and Daddy are here."

All of sudden, his eyes flew wide open, fear all over his face. "Street sweeper!" he screamed.

I assured him there was no street sweeper.

He said, "I hear it!"

Rick and I realized the hissing from the oxygen had Mason convinced the street sweeper was close and he was in imminent danger. After a short giggle between us, Rick and I reassured Mason there was not a street sweeper close by, that he was safe, and that we would not let anything happen to him.

Mason spent the night in the intensive care unit then was transferred to a regular room the next morning. He was doing well. It was painful, for sure, but the surgeon and hospital staff had a strict regimen they followed, and it worked!

However, we did find out morphine makes Mason hallucinate. Mason was gifted a Clifford the Big Red Dog mylar balloon, which we tied to the end of his bed. After being given morphine to help control the pain, Mason visualized the big red dog coming after him. Crying in fear, he yelled, "The dog is going to get me! The dog is running towards me!"

Oh my goodness! If it wasn't street sweepers, it was dogs. Everything was coming for him. Poor guy!

We had to share the room with another family. Chloe was the same age as Mason and had had the same procedure several days ago. They were anticipating being discharged the next day. With it being Mason's first day out of ICU, he was having pain as expected. He couldn't get comfortable and wasn't able to sleep.

Chloe's family was not happy with us. They would make comments from the other side of the curtain: "Please be quiet, Chloe is sleeping."

They went to the nurse to let them know how disruptive we were to their daughter, who needed her rest. Honestly, we tried to be quiet. We whispered, kept the light dim, but when you are in the same room it is utterly impossible not to disturb your roommates. The kids were just on opposite ends of their recovery. We still felt bad.

***

Ladies and gentlemen, I was tormented as a baby with the vacuum cleaner. Imagine a vacuum cleaner on steroids, then ask why I would be scared of a street sweeper coming at me. Good golly almighty, that vacuum was huge, loud, and someone was driving right toward me!

Ha! Most kids would think they would be okay because their parents would protect them from the sweeper. Not me! For all I knew, my parents had hired the street sweeper to scoop me up for surgery!

That latex balloon tied to the end of my bed? Well, the way it was swaying and moving, it made me feel like I was falling. Then, that big-ass red dog with bug eyes kept staring at me like he was chasing me into a hole.

I was frightened! Not to mention in pain and unsure what was happening to me. Having doctors, nurses, parents, grandparents, visitors, and a roommate and her family in the hospital room was very overwhelming.

I was only three years old. I wanted to run out of there. I wanted my old legs back. **I wanted to go home!**

It Takes Stitches
to Make the Quilt

Mason's initial recovery from surgery went well, and physical therapy started right away, every weekday. Since so many people had helped Mason get the therapy he needed by raising money, it felt good taking him to the appointments. It was like we were all working together as a team to get Mason stronger.

Rick took Mason to a physical therapy appointment one afternoon at the local children's hospital following his SDR. Prior to going back to the therapy room, Rick stopped into the bathroom to take care of business for the two of them.

Rick sat Mason on the toilet to urinate as this is how we always did it, so Mason felt stable. As Mason finished up, Rick raised him off the toilet, and out of nowhere, poop came out and plonked on Rick's open-toed sandal. It was not a solid bounce-off poop, but a runny soft poop. Rick was beside himself and didn't know what to do.

Eventually he was able to get Mason cleaned up and placed in his stroller, then concentrated on his foot and shoe. Water, soap, and paper towels were his only tools to use. Remarkably, he was able to get everyone cleaned up enough to still go to therapy.

***

After months of going to physical therapy an hour a day every weekday and seeing very little progress, I became disappointed. I became sad. I wasn't thrilled with what therapies were being done daily. There was a lot of Mason standing and playing with puzzles as the therapist held his knees to keep his legs straight. There was the tossing of balls while Mason side-sat and the therapist supported his core. There were reaching games to have Mason extend his arms fully. It all felt like play. Like it wasn't really helping. Like it would never get him to the place we wanted him to go.

Plus, the amount of money we were spending on the therapy was difficult for me. I felt obligated to be fiscally responsible when using the money raised for Mason's recovery and physical therapy sessions. I began to think I needed to accept Mason would not be physically as functional as I had hoped. Accept that it is what it is.

I decided to do one last look at therapy models. I began researching intensive physical therapy models. My research led us to a Miami, Florida therapy center that specialized in intense physical therapy. Their therapy model was three hours of therapy a day, five days a week, for three weeks. It isolated muscle groups and built on repetitions so specific muscles would gain strength day by day.

The model also used a Therasuit. The Therasuit was a Velcro and bungee cord "suit" that applied resistance to the child. This resistance helped to increase strength and it also acted like another set of hands for the therapist as the bungees held areas of the child the therapist couldn't. This model of therapy made sense.

Again, we, as a family, approached our local medical team to discuss the idea of traveling and doing this type of therapy. It was not well-received. The local medical team focused a lot on the Therasuit. I remember comments being made about how the suit wasn't magical and wasn't going to help your son walk.

As a parent wanting the best for your child, you must trust your gut and go with your instincts. We packed up, made arrangements with our jobs and home, and made the twenty-two-hour drive to Florida.

For three weeks, we took Mason to a physical therapy clinic every weekday. For three hours, Mason increased his strength by doing sit-ups on a gigantic ball. He did leg presses, beginning with therabands and advancing to weights. He did squats in the "magical suit," with increased resistance from the bungee cord adjustments. He did arm pulls, again starting with therabands and advancing to weights.

They used sandbags to keep his one extremity in place while he focused and strengthened the other. In case you aren't aware, when a child has spastic diplegia and tries to use one leg, the other leg can automatically kick up to try and help. Not always real safe for those around them. Ha!

The last half hour to forty-five minutes of the session, the therapist worked with Mason on functional things like sitting cross-legged, walking with his heels touching the ground, sitting with a straight back and head up, riding an adaptive bike, and even going up and down stairs. In a mere three weeks, Mason went from using his Kaye walker to tripod canes. This was after nine months of daily therapy locally with minimal results.

I will never forget the first physical therapy appointment when we got home. We were in the waiting room, and Mason's therapist came out and said, "Hey guys, welcome back. How did it go?"

We said, "Wait right there!"

Mason stood up from the waiting room chair, picked up his tripod canes, and trucked steadily over to his therapist. Her eyes were huge. Her mouth flew open. To say she was surprised was an understatement. She could not believe it. You see, prior to traveling to Shine Therapy, Mason wasn't even back in his Kaye walker full-time yet. He didn't have the strength to push through his legs to stand. We were mostly using his wheelchair. The SDR had eliminated the spasticity he used to stand, and there was no strength.

We had worked nine months in therapy to just get Mason back into his Kaye walker. Now, in only three weeks, he had bypassed his walker and was using canes!

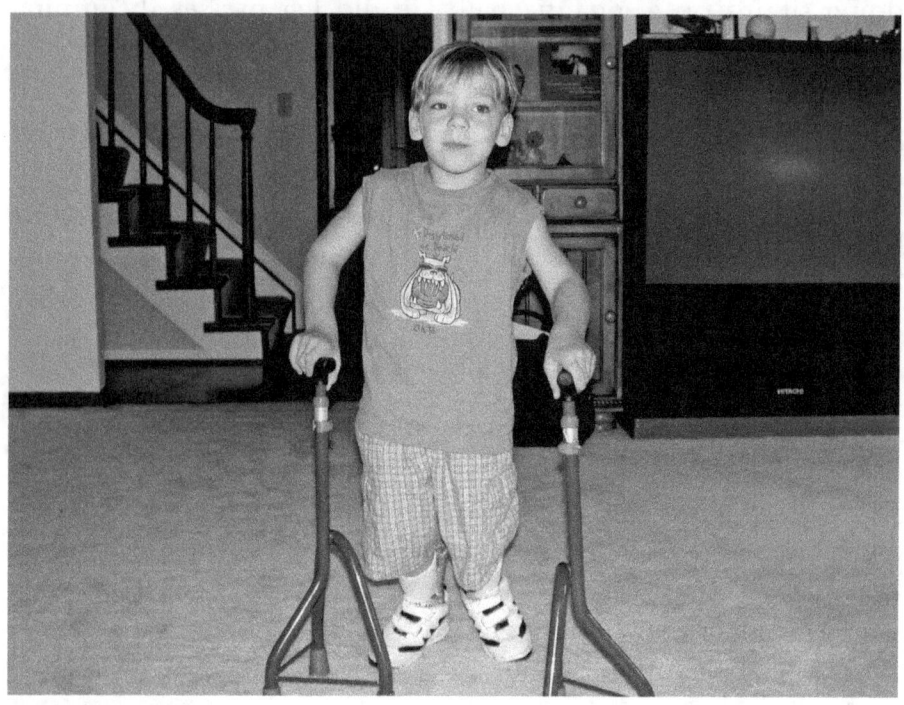

Growing up with cerebral palsy, the number one question I remember from kids and adults is "What is wrong with you?"

I never thought anything was "wrong" with me. I still don't. It was quite obvious that my legs weren't the greatest at behaving, but I was fine! I have never not known what it is like not to have cerebral palsy or not be me.

Threads interweave one another to hold the quilt together. Thread by thread. Moment by moment. Stitch by stitch. Day by day. It is all the same.

My mom found the therapy model in Florida—it was just another thread in this quilt of life. Just as she had come across the Time magazine article about SDR—another thread. Each thread provides a stitch. That article thread led to a stitch of other families and children who needed this type of surgery. The intense therapy thread helped me become stronger, then stitched new families into our lives. **Each stitch continued to interweave other squares together and this makes our quilt of life.** *How cool is that?*

That a Girl, Mom!

This triumph led Rick and I to a working relationship with the local children's hospital. They had to get this type of therapy going in the area to help children like Mason, and Mason's physical therapists agreed. We began meeting with the director of physical therapy and the powers-that-be to see how we could get this type of therapy model offered in the hospital. We were acting as a Parent Family Advisory Committee to improve care under the physical therapy umbrella.

After months and months and months of meetings, accumulating data, and doing research, the local hospital was willing to give this therapy model a try. We were so excited! However, the fiscal budget had already been submitted so they would need to wait until the following year to submit the request for training and equipment.

What? No! We don't have that kind of time. Children need this therapy now. Mason needs this therapy now. After we got over our feelings of despair, we put our problem-solving hats on and got to work. Rick and I rallied the troops; troops of fellow families whose children would benefit from this type of therapy; troops within our own family; troops of our friends, neighbors, and co-workers.

We developed a non-profit: Smiles for Kids through Suit Therapy. We had to do it that way because straight donation to the hospital would be muddy. We planned a fundraiser under the non-profit to raise monies to train the physical therapists and to purchase the equipment needed for the intense therapy model.

When you tell parents of children who have special needs that something needs to be done for their child or other children like their child, they make it happen! We made it happen in one fundraiser, which included a spaghetti dinner, a silent auction, raffles, a split-the-pot-collection, and tables where children could make crafts.

We went back to the hospital and presented them with several things. First, a check to cover the equipment, including Therasuits; second, the contact information for the therapist, who originated from Poland, to come in and do the training for their staff, paid with the fundraiser funds; and third, a request for immediate action to get things started.

Things started to move right along. Training was scheduled for therapists. An order was placed for equipment. It was happening! More excited than us were our fellow parents, as they wanted their child to experience some of the results Mason had.

After the therapists were trained and the equipment scheduled for delivery, we received a call. It was the director of physical therapy requesting to meet with us.

"Heck yeah, let's meet!" I just knew we were going to talk about ribbon-cutting, or marketing this therapy model, or gratitude to us for making this happen.

WRONG!

As we sat around the table in the conference room of the physical therapy department among our group acquired over many months, the faces were grim and defeated. The physical therapy director told us that the medical director would not allow this therapy model at the hospital due to lack of medical research. It was not an evidence-based research method.

I was livid. I asked for evidence-based research on current therapies. There weren't any. I explained this therapy method made sense. It was about the intensity of therapy, the isolation of muscle groups, and focusing on building strength in the muscles needed for better function.

Then, it came out. The problem was the Therasuit!

"What about the Therasuit?"

"There are no studies on using it, and physicians are not behind it. Ruth, Rick, the only way to move forward is to research this therapy model, and we are willing to do that."

"Uh, okay. What does that look like?"

"We accumulate clients who are willing to participate in the study. Then we perform therapy with some wearing the Therasuit during therapy, and some without."

"So, to be clear, the same amount of therapy will be done but some with a Therasuit and some without?"

"Yes."

"That doesn't make sense to me. The Therasuit is merely a piece of equipment to help the therapist work certain parts of the child's body. It is the therapy, the intensity of it, that makes the therapy work and gives the results. You will be studying the wrong thing. The study needs to be with some kids doing traditional therapy and others doing intense therapy, working towards the same goals to evaluate progress."

They were not hearing it. It was about the Therasuit and the use of it. Our donations of equipment and the Therasuits, plus the trained staff, were going to be put into a research study for one year based solely on what they wanted to study.

Talk about being stabbed in the heart. Maybe, just maybe (who am I kidding, probably not), I could have gotten past the need for research, but not when they were studying the wrong thing.

ERGH!

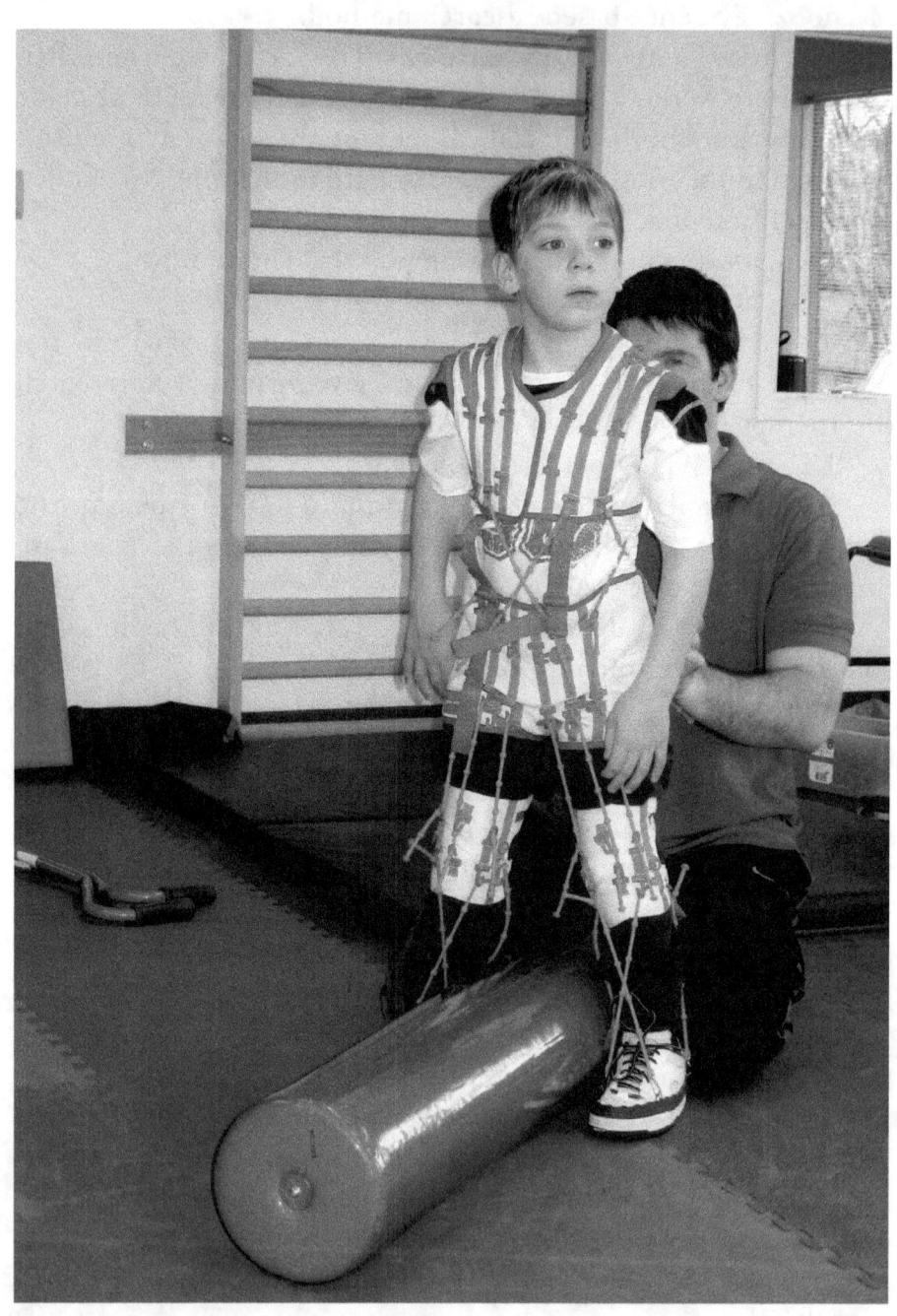

A MUDDY LIFE

My mom's research and advocacy got other parents in our area to study and consider having the selective dorsal rhizotomy surgery to increase their child's function. She helped them through insurance appeals when their insurance would not cover the surgery due to being out of state.

This is the part where I told you that things could not have been done by one person. In order to fundraise for the equipment and training of the therapists at the hospital it took a multitude of people. The rally of the troops, special needs club parents, family, friends, is what got this intense therapy model introduced to our area.

My mom felt a sense of commitment, not only to me, but to other children, to be able to give them the therapy not only that they needed following the surgery but deserved. The hospital's inability to initiate this therapy model in our area instilled a passion in my mom.

***

Have you ever heard people say that because of something happening it prevented something else from happening? For example, if so-and-so had not been running late to work, he would have been involved in an accident because that accident happened at the exact time he would have normally been at that intersection.

Well, this journey my parents were on was the same thing. All the effort, time, and work invested to get this therapy model to our area was to show them they could do it. They had what it took. The local hospital denying the Therasuit was because the Universe had other plans. It was moving my parents, especially my mom, onto another path. A path that would not have been traveled or discovered had the local hospital done the therapy exactly as she wanted. The Universe wanted to show my mom that she was stronger than she thought, more capable than she imagined, and the person needed to do what needed to be done.

***

We met with fellow families again. We were all devastated. Yet, there was some hope that families involved in bringing this model of therapy to the area would be able to participate in the study. And honestly, whether they wore or didn't wear the suit, it was going to benefit them because it was about the intensity of the therapy and isolating muscle groups!

In addition to me, there was one other mom who really, really didn't like this outcome. Our dislike was enhanced when we learned of the criteria children had to meet to participate in the research study.

Mason was out because he had recently participated in this type of therapy model already.

Children who had undergone SDRs were out.

Children who had seizures, even if controlled, were out.

Children outside a certain age range were out.

The criteria went on and on. It would be free for families, so that was a plus, but this mom and I decided the research project was not enough. If we wanted this therapy model in the area, we had to offer it!

***

Hee Hee!

Mom has never let anyone tell her "no." Fortunately, or unfortunately, I picked up on this quality. My dad will even tell you he learned really quick not to say "no" to my mom if it was something she was passionate about because a fire would be ignited and it she would become a wildfire on a mission.

You believe in something. You want something. You work for it! You go after it!

Favorite quote of my mom to this day: "If there is a will, there is a way!"

That a girl, Mom! *Watch out Cincinnati, here comes the therapy model these two badass moms know children need and deserve!*

A MUDDY LIFE

I'll just sit back and watch. Where's the popcorn?

Nose Goes

One of the more challenging things about raising Mason with his cerebral palsy was the additional equipment. Children with cerebral palsy often require orthotics known as DAFOs (dynamic ankle foot orthosis). DAFOs are custom made braces that gently hold the ankle and foot in a functional position to stand and walk. They assist in balance and proper placement of the foot. But here is the thing: Shoes are NOT made for DAFOs! It can be a week or longer process to find shoes that will work with DAFOs. If you just buy shoes in a larger size, the child ends up dragging their toes. You would think you could just buy wide-width shoes and that would do the trick. NOT! DAFOs make the child's foot not only wider, but also thicker, so even in wide shoes the braces are too thick to tie or buckle a shoe around. Let's not even talk about trying to find sandals or boots that would work with DAFOs.

Once a shoe that works is found, don't think the challenge ends there. For the parents who know, they know! The daily and sometimes more frequent escapade of putting the DAFOs on your child's feet, then wriggling, torquing, and pulling the shoe on over the brace is a workout! It is not a quick or easy process. As a family, we became efficient in getting Mason's braces and shoes on. We took turns, often playing the "Nose Goes" game to determine whose turn it was to put Mason's shoes on.

Leah's famous words echoed what we all felt at times: "Do we have to put his shoes on? Can't he just go barefoot?"

Barefoot and limited brace-wearing were options as an infant, but as Mason became a toddler and preschooler, he was too heavy to always carry. If you weren't going to carry him, he had to have his braces and shoes on to use his kaye walker.

One weekend Mason spent the night at his grandparents. His grandparents lived about thirty minutes away, so we would usually meet them halfway in a Target parking lot for the exchange. As Rick and I waited in the parking lot for his parents to come, we noticed they were significantly late, which is not like them at all. Twenty minutes after the time we said we would meet them, they pulled into the parking spot next to us. Rick's mom looked distraught. I couldn't tell if she was going to burst out laughing or burst into tears.

She said, "I'm sorry we are late. I had no idea how difficult it was to put Mason's braces and shoes on! I could not figure them out. I fought and struggled with them until I thought I would pass out. I was sweating so much. I mean, sweating more than a hot flash! Then I thought I was going to break the poor boy's ankle, so he's barefoot!"

"Uh yeah, we probably should have warned you about those!"

In addition to braces, there was Mason's kaye walker, a bag with essential things that may be needed, and Mason. As he got older, the walker became canes, and we added a wheelchair. Think of going on a vacation with little ones and how your car is stuffed from floor to ceiling with the pack-and-play, stroller, and on and on. Yup, just like that, PLUS the medical equipment. As they get older and you think you won't have to pack as much, the equipment gets larger and more cumbersome, but it's necessary for anything from quick errands to an extended trip.

A MUDDY LIFE

***

DAFOs! They are my archnemesis! They are uncomfortable. They are bulky. While I get why they are needed and they help, they also hinder and hurt! If you are not upright, you can not crawl without a lot of difficulty. Crawling was still my main way to get around when I got DAFOs, and the best way to get somewhere quickly. Think about crawling with an aircast or one of those orthopedic boots—that is what it felt like! I swear, we spent more time putting braces and shoes off and on than actually wearing them. It was always a process. A process during which I'm quite sure I learned all the cuss words out there. My parents, sister, and grandparents would express their frustration freely and vocally as they put my shoes on. Wait a minute. Just to be clear, Leah didn't cuss, just the adults. LOL!

As I got older and was growing, the DAFOs would get longer, larger, and more cumbersome. I had surgeries so my muscles would stretch, and once I had to have a tendon lengthened. After those surgeries, my foot and leg would be in perfect position, so I would balk about wearing braces. I was told braces would prevent or minimize further surgeries by maintaining the foot position.

As a teenager, I was introduced to the Noodle AFO (ankle foot orthotic). This particular brace incorporates a spiral strut, providing greater flexibility and durability than the standard carbon fiber braces. It was easier to put on, wear, and find shoes for. I wore that type of orthotics for years.

It wasn't until my late teens, early twenties, that I went to steel-toe work boots. These boots maintained my ankle support and allowed me to work sufficiently. Still can't wear sandals, and I only occasionally put on gym shoes. My work boots are my go-to. I wear them with shorts, sweatpants, and jeans. They are a little heavy, but I don't care. I'll take them over orthotics any day. I am so grateful to be out of braces!

Nose goes? Just someone get their nose over here and put my shit on!

That Was Rude, Too

One summer, we set out for Cape Cod. The whole family was going, from grandparents to cousins. We had a four-car caravan. We had stopped at McDonald's for a bathroom break and refreshment. Rick's parents graciously offered to take Mason in their SUV for the last part of the trip and they got him a strawberry milkshake to drink. It was less than an hour into the ride when they announced over the walkie-talkie: "We will need to make an emergency stop. We had an accident in the car."

Rick and I immediately looked at one another, both thinking *What now?* I quickly said, "Honey, the kid can't control his bodily functions." I just knew he had shit his pants!

Up ahead, there was a sign for a park. We pulled into the entrance. It was a big, beautiful park! There were many people there enjoying the outside, playing frisbee, walking dogs, and having picnics. Our caravan of cars pulled over into a U-shaped roundabout.

I walked back to the grandparents' car and asked, "What's wrong?"

"Mason got sick. He has thrown up all over the car!"

"Oh no!" As I leaned into the backseat to say "What's wrong, buddy?" the pungent, distinct smell of vomit filled my nose. Mason was covered from head to toe in puke. There was puke in his car seat, on the backseat of the car, and on the floor. It didn't take long to figure out the culprit of the retching massacre was the strawberry milkshake from McDonald's. He had either drank it too fast or had too much, or both. The troops went into action. Cousins were rounding up wipes. I was taking off Mason's clothes. Grandpa was looking for napkins to clean the car and car seat. My mom was trying to find new clothes for Mason in the suitcase. Leah was making sure everyone knew how gross it was and how bad it smelled.

I finally got all of Mason's clothes off and yelled to Rick to come to the other side of the car to get Mason while I got my bearings. As I pulled Mason out of the car butt-ass naked and turned around to hand the dangling boy to his dad, a horse-drawn carriage went by with a bride, groom, and the wedding party. I mean, right there, right next to us! While I was handing the naked boy off to my husband, the bride and I locked eyes. It was a standstill moment. One of those moments that feels like an hour but is merely a few minutes.

Without missing a beat, Rick blurted out, "Well, we provided them with a birth control message."

Our group erupted into embarrassed, then hysterical laughter. We changed Mason's clothes, got the car cleaned up as well as we could, and got the heck out of dodge.

We still talk about that trip to this day and what an embarrassing experience it was.

Six years later, Rick's parents were cleaning out their car to trade it in for a new car and I received a phone call from Rick's mom. She said, "You aren't going to believe this. I was sweeping out the crevices of the seats in the back of my car and there were still pink flakes from where Mason puked going to Maryland!"

Good grief!

***

Hey! I'm not going to pass up a milkshake! I'm all about food, drink, and entertainment! There is not much to do in a car for hours and hours. If I can slurp down a milkshake to pass the time on a car ride, bring it on! I really don't know what happened. After I drank the shake, my stomach started not to feel well and out it came. I felt so much better after it came out but it was pretty stinky after that. Mamaw and Pappaw rolled their windows down and opened my windows in the back halfway. The breeze felt nice, and it even helped to blow the vomit out of my hair and down into the car seat.

It was quite a ruckus, and I wasn't sure what the big deal was. I puked, let's move on, people.

I remember the horses. As mom was handing me off to my dad, I reached out and was saying horses, horses! No one was paying attention to me, and they certainly were not allowing me to look at the horses. Daddy turned me around so I was facing the car, and I thought that was so rude! **But I interrupted their wedding procession, so I guess that was rude, too.**

Just the Universe
Running Its Course

Raising Leah and Mason was challenging!

The special needs arena was a whole new ballgame. It was taking us in directions we had no idea we would be taking. We were learning about cerebral palsy and its ramifications daily. We were becoming advocates and spearheading new treatments for the area. We met so many different people, from professionals to fellow parents.

I was blessed to be able to work part-time as a nurse so I could take care of Leah and Mason. But still, it was a lot!

So, imagine our surprise when I became pregnant! I'm not going to lie—I had the ultimate meltdown.

First, let's address the obvious. Pregnancies don't just happen. As an educated adult and nurse, I know how it happens. So, why was I surprised? I was on birth control. However, I was being treated for a urinary tract infection and the antibiotics affected the effectiveness.

Voila! PREGNANT!

Why did I melt down? Where do I begin? I re-lived Mason's pregnancy, all the misdiagnoses, all the appointments, the fear, the unknown. I screamed at Rick that there was absolutely no way

I was going to be able to take care of an infant and Mason and Leah. Rick lovingly assured me we would get through it. We would make it work. Even with his calm demeanor and reassurance, I felt hesitation and fear.

Then I went into "OMG! What if this baby has special needs? What if I have two children with special needs? OMG! What if I have twins again? Even worse, what if I lose this baby during the pregnancy, like I lost Jackson?"

It was a snowball rolling down a hill and quickly becoming an avalanche.

As the weeks went by, I calmed down by convincing myself the baby was a girl. I had it in my head that Leah's pregnancy was uneventful and went smoothly, and that this one was going to be too, because it was a girl. Crazy, right? It was the only thing that helped me at the time. I was an emotional disaster until I breathed into a girl, and therefore a smooth pregnancy. We all know the gender of the pregnancy didn't cause the complications—it was the twins.

"Twin pregnancies put you at risk for double complications." I've heard you a trillion times, Dr. Maggie!

I put that whole thought and well-worn saying out of my mind. Our sweet baby girl was going to be named Jenna Ruth Bailey. We were going to do this. We were going to make it!

So, imagine our surprise at the twenty-week ultrasound when they announced, "You're having a boy!"

Rick very loudly said, "There is only one, right?"

With a giggle, the ultrasound technician replied, "Yes, there is only one."

I came to terms with having a boy. Honestly, the gender wasn't important to me, I had just convinced myself Leah's pregnancy was smooth because she was a girl. Of course, we were told she was a boy in the beginning, so my whole gender theory thing was all in my head. My pregnancy continued without any incidents. Our anxieties diminished with each reassuring obstetrician appointment.

Our baby boy was growing, rocking the ultrasounds, and no alarms were triggered.

On January 28, 2005, Rick and I welcomed healthy, beautiful, perfect Quinn Michael Bailey into our family. Leah was nine years old and in fourth grade; Mason was six years old and starting kindergarten. Our family was now complete, and our hearts were full.

Go ahead, Mom, blame the antibiotics, but I know it was just the Universe playing out its course. Quinn was chosen for our family. He was meant to be.

People want to believe they have control, but the truth is they don't. We can try. We can plan. We can go in certain directions, but our course is in motion. The spiritual world is a powerful, unconditionally loving world. It has the divine good in place for all.

Don't get me wrong. There is evil. People can live in darkness and try to expend that darkness into others' lives in so many formats. There is free will where we get to make our own decision and choices. Free will and darkness intertwined can have horrific outcomes. But when we ask ourselves, "what lesson can be learned?" "What is this experience trying to teach me?" "How can I bring light to this darkness?" It makes earthly living brighter.

We are all experiences. We are here to share our stories. Our experiences may heal others. Our spirits embrace this quest.

When people die, many get enthralled with how the person died, especially if it is a traumatic death such as a car accident. Precious memories get fogged by the way they died versus the way they lived. In my opinion, the truth is that when we die, we leave our physical bodies, that's it. It is like going to sleep. Our conscious does not die, it merely transitions to the next realm.

As I've heard at many International Association Near Death Studies (IANDS) conferences, I have attended, people say they did not realize that they were dead. It took time to realize they were looking down on their body on the operating table or the place of their passing. Again, this is because spiritually, we are the same. Our bodies are vessels carrying our consciousness. When our bodies are born or die we still remain whole in spirit.

Oops, sorry, I didn't mean to off-rail and go down the death road. But birth and death go hand in hand.

***

It was the spring before Mason was to start kindergarten. We decided to do a kindergarten visit to see how the classroom setting worked and what it would be like.

Mrs. Rawlins was more than willing to have us visit. We arrived during reading circle and when we walked in the students got really quiet. Mrs. Rawlins welcomed us in. Immediately, the children started to ask questions. "What's wrong with his legs?" "What happened?"

We explained there were medical complications in the pregnancy, and he was born with a condition called cerebral palsy or CP. We explained that it affects how his legs work, but he was still just like them!

At that visit, who should we see? The janitors! Mason immediately froze and the color drained from his face.

Mom mode! How do I overcome these challenges for my sweet boy? I decided to write a children's book that explained Mason so the kindergarten teacher could read it the first day of school to the other students. I was trying to nip the questions and uncertainty in the bud.

As far as the janitors, we held a janitor summer luncheon! I made a picnic lunch and took it to them, and we all sat around and ate, talked, and introduced Mason. It was a first for them! No one had ever wanted to meet or picnic with them before. We had a great time, and Mason seemed relieved to have met them.

Momma got to do what a momma got to do!

***

My mom is simply the best. She would do anything and everything to help me, to make things easier for me, and to help the world feel more comfortable around me.

I loved the janitor luncheon! It made me feel so much more comfortable around them and not so scared.

Thank you, mom, and thank you, universe for running your course.

All Jobs for Superman

It was Mason's first day of kindergarten. He was using his tripod canes to walk into the building from the bus. All the other students walked around on the sidewalk to enter the building, but due to distance and ease, Mason chose to cut across the grass that led right into his classroom. I was walking alongside him. Envision a slow, but steady, Mason procession toward his classroom.

Well, not unusual and certainly expected, Mason fell! His feet or legs did not do as they were supposed to and the next thing you know, he is sprawled across the grass. It was a gentle fall, so I wasn't concerned. I kept walking, but slowly, as I knew it would take him time to get up and restart.

Out of nowhere, a mom comes running to Mason's rescue! "Is he alright? Is he okay?"

I giggled and said, "He's fine." I was befuddled by her excitement. You see, this was an occurrence that happened A LOT!

Then, she reached down, put her hands out, and said to Mason, "Here, let me help you up."

Out of nowhere, and deep down from my toes, I yelled "NO!"

The woman jumped up from being hunched over to help Mason. Her face said, "WTF lady?"

I realized my stern "no" and nonchalant behavior over Mason's tumble was not being well-received. I began to explain I wasn't trying to be mean, but merely trying to help Mason help himself. I explained that if I helped Mason up every time he fell, he would never learn how to get up on his own, and that I or someone else may not always be there when he fell.

She stared at me, and her eyes spoke the words she never said: "He is just a baby. He is struggling. I don't believe you, lady, you are a horrible person!"

And off she went, head down, shuffling through the grass, and mad as hell!

As crazy and absurd as it may seem, I take pride in this. Don't get me wrong, I have helped Mason more times than you can count in his lifetime. Sometimes due to convenience, sometimes due to time constraints, sometimes due to injury, and sometimes just because he asked.

Mrs. Rawlins read our book, Why Do You Walk with Canes, You Ask, to the classroom. She said the students were nonchalant and didn't seem interested in it. It was if they accepted him right away and didn't need an explanation. I'm not sure if it was because he had some students he knew from preschool in his class, or if it was because they all started the same day so everyone was new.

Unlike the book, the friendship with the janitors was needed. It helped to relieve his anxiety regarding their presence. That was a momma win!

***

I loved my lil guy in jeans! I felt they made him look so handsome! It wasn't long into kindergarten when the school occupational therapist mentioned maybe I should put Mason in sweatpants. She explained that by having Mason wear sweatpants, he would be able to become more independent and not require as much help while using the restroom. She continued to tell me how hard the zipper and button on the jeans were for Mason to do. I heard what she was saying, and I appreciated it, but I couldn't let my handsome denim-wearing boy go. I loved him in jeans!

One morning as I was getting things ready for school, Mason was in his room playing with his toys. Out of nowhere, I heard a scream.

I ran into his room, and he was sitting up against the wall. He was cackling, "I did it! I did it! I put my own jeans on!"

He had heard the occupational therapist talk about him wearing jeans to school. He was determined to prove her wrong. He was so proud of himself, as was I. This was no easy task to say the least. He told me he got the idea when I left him to go get breakfast ready and that he had been working on it the whole time. He explained how hard it was and that his legs did not want to cooperate, but he made them!

We were so happy!

It is times like these that you can't help but celebrate and be happy for the accomplishment. It is also the time that gets you in the gut because your child shouldn't have to work so hard for such a simple thing and be six years old before he can do it!

Sniffle.

***

Mason was in afternoon kindergarten. A group of us decided to go out to lunch before drop-off. The group going to lunch included me, Mason, my niece, her husband Shane, and Mason's kindergarten teacher, Mrs. Rawlins whom we had befriended.

After lunch, my niece and I had an appointment to go get our nails done at the salon next to the restaurant. Shane graciously volunteered to take Mason to school for me.

My niece and I had been in the salon for over a half an hour when the owner of the salon came back to the table I was at and in his Vietnamese accent said, "Ruth?"

"Yes."

"You need to leave and go get your son."

I giggled and said, "No, my son is with my nephew."

He got a little panicky and said, "No, you do not understand, your son—he missin'!"

I sincerely believed there was a language barrier happening. "No, he is not missing. He is at school."

"His teacher called, he is not at school. He missin'."

This got my attention since I had just left lunch with his teacher. She knew I was getting my nails done. The school was only a few blocks from the restaurant. Mason should have been there a long time ago. My mind raced. They had to have been in a wreck! I called my nephew's phone immediately.

"Hello?"

"Shane? Where are you?"

"I'm at Mason's school. Why?"

"Where's Mason? His teacher called and said he wasn't in class."

"We're sitting in the car waiting for class to start."

"To start? It started thirty minutes ago!"

In the background, I heard Mason's cackling laughter. Come to find out Mason told Shane school didn't start until one, instead of twelve thirty. Shane even asked Mason who kept coming out of his classroom looking around. Mason explained that it was "just a paraprofessional" who was probably looking for a student.

SHE WAS! She wasn't "just" a paraprofessional—she was Mason's paraprofessional. She WAS looking for a student . . . Mason!

Shane took Mason into class and explained what happened. Ms. Mass was not happy. She had gotten herself worked up and, just like me, had thought something bad had happened. Shane was so embarrassed that he had let a six-year-old play him like that. He apologized profusely to Ms. Mass and Mrs. Rawlins. He then bowed his head down and shuffled to his car. I made Mason write an apology note to Ms. Mass.

***

As far as falling on my way into kindergarten, I was going to milk it. I was going to let that caring young mother help me right up. I laid in the grass and batted my eyelashes, allowing her to think I was helpless.

However, when I looked over at my mom and saw her "It AIN'T happening" look, I started to flip over and push myself up.

I had just learned how to walk with tripod canes. Walking with them was going well, but the falling and getting up, that was hard!

My mom knew I needed to learn. She knew it would take practice. And I knew she was right. So, I struggled through and got up.

Just like my mom to ruin all my fun.

***

Oh my gosh, Shane and Ms. Mass! One of my ultimate pull-offs!

Hey, I went to school, but I really didn't like it, even in kindergarten. I knew what time school started. I knew Ms. Mass was looking for me when Shane asked. I was just enjoying my time talking to Shane in the car. We were laughing and having a good time until my mom called and ruined it! Everyone was so upset. I didn't understand why, I thought it was a great prank.

Yeah, my mom made me write an apology note, but you know what I told her? "If I must write an apology note then I think Shane should too. He is the grown-up here. I can't help it if he believed a six-year-old."

The next day, I took our apology notes to school—one from me and one from Shane!

The summer of kindergarten we felt Mason needed another round of intense physical therapy.

We found a clinic near Detroit. It was much closer than Miami, but still required three weeks away from home. Rick and I had to joggle vacation time to make it work. My friend, Annie, was willing to go up with me for one of the weeks when Rick came home.

After a three-hour therapy session, Mason, Annie, and I came back to the hotel, had dinner, and relaxed with some cartoons. Towards evening, I wanted Mason to take a bath and he was not having it. After several calm, soothing, "you can't stink" conversations, I felt that I was just going to have to make him take one.

Mason got so angry with me. He started screaming and crying. In the midst of his tantrum, he spouted off: "You're a bbbb . . . bbbbbb . . ."

His stuttering B took Annie and I by surprise, and we both waited for what we knew was not going to be nice.

"You're a BBBBBB-EAGLE!"

We all died laughing. That certainly wasn't the word we thought was going to come out of his mouth!

The third week of intense therapy was really taking it out of Mason. He was tired. He was sore. He just did not want to do anymore. It is hard watching your six-year-old struggle through exercises. It takes a toll on your heart that you are here pushing your kiddo so he can improve functionally, when all you really want is for him to be able to go outside and play on the playground. Then there is the expense. Not only the expense of the therapy program, but the expense of travel, which includes gas, hotel, food, and activities for three weeks. So, when Mason was tired, sore, and not wanting to do the work on a given day, I would think we're not getting our "money's worth" for the time there. I kept pushing and pushing him, explaining he was in the last week and he could do it!

As he cried and the therapists patiently continued to work with him, I took a walk outside. The therapy center was in a plaza, and at the end was a police station. I went into the station and asked the officers if they would be willing to come talk to my son and encourage him to continue to work hard and become stronger. They were more than happy to.

When those two police officers walked into the therapy center, Mason's face went white! His tears dried up, his crying stopped, and he was looking for the closest door.

The officers were so kind. "Hey buddy, what are you doing there?"

A soft, almost inaudible "nothing" came out of Mason's lips.

"We are super proud of you for doing all this hard work. It is going to make you stronger. You know, as police officers, we must do a lot of hard work. There is a training that we have to complete before we can patrol the streets."

"Uh huh." Sniffle, sniffle.

"Well, you keep up the good work. We came over to root you on as we know how difficult it can get. You have a great day, buddy."

"Okay."

"No more tears, Okay?"

"Okay officers," he exhaled softly.

The rest of the day, Mason worked the hardest he had ever worked in therapy. He asked on multiple occasions, "Are those police officers going to come back?"

"No honey, they are not going to come back."

Having stayed at the same hotel for three weeks, we ended up meeting a pilot from Germany. His name was Trey. He was in his late twenties or early thirties and quickly became friends with six-year-old Mason around the pool table. They would bounce balls off the rim of the table and laugh if any of the balls went into the pouch.

Trey's primary language was German, so his English was broken, but he and Mason developed a cool friendship.

One day amidst pool play, Trey asked about the type of therapy Mason did and what it did for him. We invited Trey to come to therapy with us the next day. He was excited to attend. That excitement quickly diminished when we walked into the therapy center to find children crying while doing therapy. Trey could not and was not willing to understand why the children were in cages with bungees, wearing suits (Therasuits), and more importantly screaming and crying. He was distraught. He thought it was the most horrible thing he had ever seen! He left as quick as he came.

Evenings were a little different around the pool table after that. He and Mason still shared a friendship and played pool games, but there was an uncomfortable tension in the air.

Honestly, seeing it from his view, with an unfamiliarity with children who must do physical therapy, it probably did look like a torture chamber. Hell! I know parents, including me, would prefer not to have their children there working so hard to just increase function and possibly gain more independence. It wasn't our favorite thing to put our child through or watch either.

Intense physical therapy was HARD! I was six years old and doing three hours of therapy every day, five days a week. My muscles hurt. I was tired. I did not want to do this hard work every day. I wanted to be a kid. I wanted to play, be read to, and watch cartoons.

The weeks of therapy were wearing on me. When my mom wanted me to take a bath, I did not want to! I wanted to have some control over something. I sure wasn't having control over my body, or about doing therapy. They didn't care what I thought. They believed it was what was best for me, so I was going. So not taking a bath—I thought I could try to control that at least.

My mom was not giving up though. It made me so mad! I could feel the rage within my body. You're dang right I wanted to say something other than "beagle," but I didn't.

Another method of fear for me to oblige was bringing the police officers into the physical therapy center. I get what they were trying to do, but at the same time, I was a little kid! They were very nice and did help me to want to work harder and be strong.

It was at this point in my life that I began to identify more and more with fear. The fear of loud noises, fear of authority, fear of not being able to do things like other kids, fear of not being loved, fear of not being worthy or accepted because of my disability. It was also at this age that I began to feel more distanced from my spiritual side. I was still able to sense others' comfort or discomfort with me and my disability. I could still read the energy in the room. But I was becoming overwhelmed and confused. I was questioning where I belonged in this world. What more could I do to teach? What was my purpose? I knew the Universe would give me what I needed; it had up to this point, but I could not stop the questioning.

***

I had a knack for making friends anywhere I went. It was a magnetic attraction that I still have to this day.

Trey was no different. I won him over in the game room around the pool table. I was intrigued by his German accent, and when I found out he was a pilot I couldn't quit asking questions. We made each other's light shine brighter. He taught me about planes and being a pilot, and I taught him about cerebral palsy and perseverance. It was a learning and growing experience.

I didn't understand why Trey thought the therapy for children who had cerebral palsy was so repulsive, although I can see how it looked scary, like my mom said. I tried to tell him I was fine, and that the therapy really was not that bad. I didn't want it to affect our friendship, but ultimately it did. Trey and I used to write letters when we both parted from Michigan, but after Trey visited the therapy center with us, his letters stopped coming. I still wonder what he is up to.

Falling and getting up, pushing through intense therapies, pulling off pranks, and smiling through the policemen visits—all jobs for Superman!"

Sprinkle of Awareness

My unexpected pregnancy and birth of my sweet newborn did not stop my efforts to bring intense therapy to the tri-state area. My fellow parent, Lila, and I continued to research, work with other therapy centers who offered intense therapy, and explore spaces to have the center. Lila and I shared a bond. A bond of knowing, since we both had sons with similar challenges, a bond of passion to make things better and share with others, and a bond of realizing that if we want something done, we have to do it! We began hiring and training physical therapists and finally got a loan from a bank (that was quite the task for two women embarking on a "high-risk" venture).

In 2008, we opened our own physical therapy center, LBT It was a self-paid clinic offering individualized therapy programs, including intensive therapy utilizing the Therasuit method. We were the 109th center in the United States to offer this type of therapy.

Our center was in the building of the park district. It was a room the park district used as a vending machine room. They were gracious enough to lease the space to us for therapy. Ironically, LBT treated more self-paying clients in a year than the local hospital did in their free research study. Their criteria for children to participate in the study was just too stringent.

The theory behind LBT and intense models was, and still is, to gain strength initially through three to four weeks of therapy, maintain strength through a home program and fitness, and live life without running to appointments every week. In this model, children only have follow-up visits every three to four months, maybe even six months, depending on the child's age, ability, diagnosis, and stamina.

At LBT, we saw children take their first steps. We saw children ride adaptive bikes. We saw their function improve immensely. We offered fitness classes to children wanting to maintain their strength.

The board of the park district invited Lila and I to attend one of their monthly meetings. They wanted us to introduce ourselves, explain LBT and how it worked. We were excited for this opportunity. We met all the executive board members, some volunteers, and other employees. It was a decent amount of people. Lila did an amazing job explaining LBT and how and why it was important for us to open a center in our area. She explained how hard the therapy was for kiddos, but the benefits they reaped were worth it. After she got done talking, we asked if anyone had any questions.

One board member spoke up. "I have noticed your therapists bringing some of the kids out into the hallway to attempt to walk or ride an adaptive bike. Don't you think it would be better if "these" kids were kept in your room?"

I was taken aback. The way this question was asked was not kind. It was condescending and it did not sit well with me. But giving him the benefit of the doubt, I inquired more.

"What do you mean?"

"I mean, there are other children from classes and camp that go up and down the hallways. I think that "your" children can be a hindrance or in their way."

W . . . the actual . . . F?

Lila and I exchanged looks. Who was going to respond? My look said, "Oh honey, I will!"

"'These' children are just like 'those' children. They are working hard to be able to do things like the other children. They want to be included and around other children. It is important for children and the world to interact with children who were born with challenges and special needs. We are all the same, just given different challenges."

"Yeah, I know but I still think it would be safer and better if they stayed in the room."

I could feel the heat in my body. I wanted to be kind, but I also wanted to lay into him. And why do people always use the words "safe" and "unsafe" when they're uncomfortable among people who have a disability? I ended with, "With all due respect, sir, I hope that if you or a significant loved one ever end up having a stroke and going into a rehabilitation center for therapy that they keep you in your room and not allow you or your loved ones to have interactions with others!"

He responded, "That is different. I would still be among my kind in the hallway."

"Are you kidding me? KIND? Sir, do you not understand we are all human beings? All human beings that have our own battles to fight?"

The room got quiet. The executive director thanked Lila and I for coming and explaining our mission and expressed his gratitude for having us as tenants.

My heart was scarred. The member of our park district didn't want us to have our patients among their typical clients. What in the world? It is eye-opening when you are in a place where you think you are among others who understand, only to find out they really don't.

Sigh!

***

Remember my parents getting the sprinkle of awareness from the child in the wheelchair during the walks they used to take? It is very possible that the park district members were getting their sprinkle of awareness from the therapy center being in their building. That sprinkle could revisit them as they left the parking lot, or it could have shown up years later, like my mom's did.

This is what I mean by sometimes you can look back and see why things happened and other times you may not. We will probably never know if that conversation Lila and my mom had at that meeting had an impact or not on the members around that table.

Regardless, it was a sprinkle of awareness.

I Wasn't the One Who Peed My Pants

The summer when Mason was eight years old, we took a family trip to Orlando. We had purchase an "On-the-go" card, which is where you pay a certain amount and it allows you to go on any of the listed attractions on the card.

We went on a boat that toured the waters of elegant, extraordinarily large homes. They were homes of well-to-do people, even celebrities. In the middle of the tour, it started to downpour. The tour was cut short. The boat docked and we had to gather our things and make it to the car. Things such as Mason, stroller, walker, Quinn, and all the other people and things Rick and I were responsible for.

Back in the car, we were all trying to dry off and wait out the torrential rain and storms.

It was at that time Mason declared, "I have to pee! I can't hold it either!"

I looked Rick and he said, "He is going to have to wait. I am not getting out in this storm."

"Mom, I can't wait! I can't wait!"

At that moment, I spotted a water bottle. A sixteen-ounce, buy-in-the-store water bottle.

I excitedly said, "We will just have to use this!"

My mom, who was sitting in the passenger seat next to me, said, "I don't think that is going to work."

"Sure it will. We will make it work."

Rick blurted out, "No! We are not doing that. That is a disaster in the making."

"I can't wait! I can't wait!"

I told Rick and my mom to help Mason with his pants. I opened the water bottle, cracked the window, and poured the leftover water out. Mason was standing between the seats butt naked, with Rick in the back holding him upright. I took his little penis and pointed it into the water bottle. Holding it securely, I announced it was safe for him to go.

As he began urinating, the force of the urine caused his penis to come out of the water bottle, and although I still had a hold of it, it was like a sprinkler system going off in the car. My mom was screaming as she got peed on. Rick was disgusted because he knew it was not a good idea. Pee was going everywhere! Ceiling, dashboard, my mom.

I got to laughing so hard I couldn't control myself. And when I say laughed so hard I couldn't control myself, I mean, actually control myself! I ended up full-blown peeing my pants from laughing! We would have been better off getting wet out in the rain than in the car with pee!

After the commotion and rain settled, we traveled to the nearest Target to get dry clothes for me. In the parking lot, I started to explain to Rick what I needed, like underwear, leggings, and the sizes. My go-with-the-flow husband was not having it. This is one of he few times that I remember in which is adamantly was not going to help with the solution. That little turkey REFUSED to go in Target for me. He said he told me that it would be a disaster and I didn't listen.

He said, "You peed your pants, not me!"

"What? Are you kidding me? I can't go in there with pee pants on!"

"I don't know what to tell you."

I looked at my mom who merely shrugged her shoulders with a giggle.

I found a light windbreaker in the car, tied it around my waist, and headed into Target to get me some fresh undies and pants. A girl has to do what a girl has to do!

Just for the record, Rick may not have gone into Target, but while I was in there, he cleaned up the car with baby wipes and towels. Even in those "stand his ground" moments, Rick always comes around and would do anything for anyone, especially for me and his kids. He is truly a saint and the love of my life.

***

I am sorry to be so bold right now, but did my mom say "my little penis"? My eight-year-old penis may not have been fully up to its potential size, but I can tell you it was bigger than a throwaway water bottle opening. I mean, c'mon!

My mom and I are known for our shenanigans. We try to make things work no matter what. I didn't care what she tried, I wanted to pee! If the water bottle option was going to allow me to do that, I was all for it!

When, she said, "Okay, go!" I did! I peed high. I peed low. I peed this way and that way. I peed until I could pee no more. Immediate relief.

Hey, I wasn't the one who peed in MY pants!

Everything Happens for a Reason

LBT was growing, but it was difficult for families to afford the treatment. Honestly, it was heart-wrenching to ask families to pay out-of-pocket. We were one of those families. We knew the expense of treatments, therapies, and other medical costs. We were fortunate enough to have benefited from this model through the generous donations of family, friends, co-workers, neighbors, and strangers. But the donations were only going to last for a short period of time in the scheme of Mason's life and need for long-term therapy.

After several years, my fellow mom and co-founder of LBT decided to resign her position and spend more time with her family. I had to decide either to give up on the business or find someone else to help me. I knew I couldn't do it alone. I had the passion, enthusiasm, and spunk, even the medical understanding, but I lacked the business and marketing expertise, which was essential if I wanted LBT to succeed.

My mother-in-law suggested I meet with a family friend who ran a successful business to see if she could help or would want to be part of LBT. I was hesitant, as her business was in residential and commercial equipment, far from meeting the needs of special needs children. But her business was strong and successful, and as my mother-in-law reminded me, I didn't go into the therapy business knowing all there was to know about it—I learned it.

So we met. It was an incredible meeting. She was smart, strong, and passionate. It was immediately apparent that she could help run the business and wanted to help meet the needs of the children. She stated that business partnership is like a marriage, you relish in the success and work through the hard stuff together. Under her mentorship, LBT began to get insurance contracts so we could see more children. We got the business loan paid off in record time, grew our staff, and moved to an expansive facility. All these things happened because Janie stepped in and put her business expertise to work. And as the therapy center business model grew, so did our friendship.

It was so much fun being co-owners of LBT. I have never had a person who had my back like that before. I never had someone encourage me, empower me, and build my confidence the way she did. She helped me get through the challenging times and celebrated the best times. In addition to the business aspect, she was there to help me through so many challenges with Mason, from school and medical decisions to surgeries, and therapies. Like me, she didn't take "no" for an answer. She agreed with my beloved statement, "If there is a will, there is a way." We shared a zillion laughs, trips, and made memories that will always remain.

The happiness of walking into the new, expanded therapy center every morning to the brightest lime green walls with accents of ocean blue was indescribable. I loved that center! I loved the people who worked there. I loved the families and children I met. I loved the relationships I built. I relished in so many accomplishments our clients achieved. I still love the memories made. You've probably heard the saying, "If you love what you do, you will never work a day in your life." This was the first time I understood what that really meant.

It was hard work! Not only for the children working out three hours a day, five days week, but also for the staff working with them, and us behind the scenes. It was endless, trying to make ends meet, to keep staff happy, to maintain standards, and to grow. Everyone worked hard.

There was a heap of challenges, including writing contracts for insurance coverage, appealing insurance denials, withholding government standards, staying up to date on therapy methodologies, paying for more and more equipment, managing schedules, incorporating volunteers, writing grants, and maintaining medical records for compliance.

In addition to the successes mentioned above, we also developed the LBT Adaptive Bike Center. Through the center, we were able to get over one hundred children on adaptive bikes, mostly through grants and resources for funding. The price for these bikes was outrageous, coming in around five thousand dollars per bike. We also hosted vendor fairs, speakers, and events to bring education and awareness to families and the community.

Although the expenses were high compared to the profits, the center managed. Janie and I never took a salary or drew from LBT for our personal accounts. The only draws taken went to Mason's needs for his therapy, or equipment that wasn't covered by his insurance. Janie and I aspired to get to the point where the center could pay us. I had hoped to have LBT as my only job and be able to leave the hospital, but that never happened.

**

See! By the hospital not accepting the Therasuit in the therapy model, it spun my mom in another direction.

Universe.

Of course, no one knows why when things happen, but everything does happen for a reason. I know people hate that saying. Some even get angry because it is so devastating to hear, especially if it is said about the loss of a loved one. I get it. Some earthly lessons just plain suck! Life and its lessons aren't easy. Ask me and I will tell you, my life is not easy—but I'm here.

Sometimes in life we learn why we had to endure the loss, go through the challenge, suffer through the struggle, and sometimes we don't. **Moment to moment, thread to thread, everything happens for a reason, sometimes beyond our understanding while in physical form.**

FREEEEEEDOM!

Since Mason was limited with mobility, motorized toys were a dream. They gave him such freedom. He loved them! His grandparents were absolute rockstars when it came to giving Mason motorized toys for holidays or his birthdays.

As he grew, so did the battery-operated toys, and the speed of them increased. The motorized toy car in preschool became a motorcycle, then a John Deere tractor, then a battery-operated ATV.

When he got older, his dad would ride him on the riding lawn mower (I know, unsafe, should not have, and really don't think I would do it now due to safety reasons, but we did it then). Mason thought it was the coolest thing ever. Around the age of nine, Mason began using the mower by himself to cut our grass. He also got his first gas-powered ATV.

Mason loved being outside. He loved the dirt and getting muddy.

One warm spring day, Mason ventured outside. Before too long, we saw him with one of Rick's handsaws cutting off a tree branch hanging down low enough for him to reach.

GOOD GRIEF!

Rick and I waited for the day Job and Family Services (JFS) would show up at our door asking what kind of parents let their handicapped son use a saw and gas-powered equipment.

We just wanted him to do as much as any other boy would do.

***

Let's talk about battery-operated riding toys! **FREEEEEDOM!**

The one thing about getting around as a child was how slow I always was. Everything took effort, time, and concentration. When I sat on a battery-operated toy and pressed the button, joy encompassed my whole being! I no longer had a disability. I no longer had any worries. I was a boy with a toy, enjoying life!

That day when my next toy was a gas-powered ATV . . . HONEY! There was no holding me back! My parents were extremely strict about speed (they governed the engine, ergh!), and I had rules I had to follow. Believe me, I was following them, because I didn't want this freedom and fun to be taken away. I wore that helmet. I stayed behind that certain tree in our yard. I only rode it when they were supervising. Whatever they wanted me to do, I did.

I just wanted to be able to ride.

As far as cutting tree branches goes—I had to find things to do! I had one arm on the branch and the other hand held the saw. I felt balanced and safe.

I Hate It When My Mom Is Right

Independently using our riding lawn mower and cutting our yard was the highlight of Mason's week. He would go to the garage, prop his canes up on the wall, get on the mower, turn the key, and off he'd go. Week after week, he would cut our grass and be in all his glory.

One day, Rick and I were in the living room, windows open, enjoying an iced tea. Mason had cut the front yard and had gone to the back. We did not think a thing of it. Well, after a while, we looked out our front bay window, and there was Mason. He had the steps to the plastic slide from our playset in front of him, and he was using them as his walker.

Rick and I went flying outside. "What happened?"

Mason explained the mower shut off. He said he yelled for us, and even for our neighbor, Bob, but no one heard him. He said he wasn't sure what to do, so he slid off the mower onto the ground. He crawled his way over to the plastic slide, removed the stairs, and used them as his walker to get us.

OMG! We didn't know whether to laugh or cry. Such a creative solution, and Mason was unphased by the whole incident.

Once again, Rick and I were like, "Uh, are we bad parents?"

Job and Family Services—they're coming!

***

We had a neighbor who was a paraprofessional at Mason's preschool and elementary school. Her name was Laney and she worked with one of Mason's friends, Heather, who was visually impaired. Laney hired Mason to cut her grass weekly. It was his first paying job, and he was so proud to have it!

Mason cut Laney's grass for years and years until she retired and moved out of the neighborhood. Her reaching out to Mason, her trust in him and the friendship she developed with him, will always stay close to our hearts.

***

One day, I was cutting the grass and the mower conked out on me in the backyard. I yelled for my parents. I yelled for our neighbor. I could tell no one was coming. I wasn't hurt, I was just "stuck." My extra legs, aka canes, were in the garage where I had gotten on the mower.

Dag! **I hate it when my mom is right.** *She said I had to learn how to get up in case one day no one was there to help me when I fell. This wasn't a fall, but it certainly was a situation. I was stranded.*

As I scoured the yard with my eyes, I saw the plastic playset. The steps to the slide looked like a walker to me. I slithered down off the mower, dissected the slide, and made my way to the front of the house.

And for the record, if JFS had come to our house, I would not have let them take my parents, my motorized toys, the lawn mower, or any tools. I would have turned into the Tasmanian Devil and scared them off!

***

It was during my time of cutting Laney's yard that I experienced a voice while mowing. The voice said, "Mason," and that was it.

I knew the voice immediately. It was my brother, Jackson. I felt his presence as I continued to mow. I remember telling my mom I talked to Jackson that day, and she nonchalantly said, "Oh really, what did you talk about?"

"Well, we didn't really talk. I felt his presence and he said 'Mason.' That was it."

"That's nice dear," she responded.

I could tell it wasn't that she didn't believe me, but rather she didn't know what to do or say about it.

I felt reassured because I had been losing that close relationship with my brother the older I got, and I didn't like it.

Lifetime of Lessons

The passing of the Affordable Care Act (ACA) in 2015 affected Leap Beyond Therapy's ability to provide therapy to children with neuromuscular disorders. ACA made reimbursement rates lower, which meant we couldn't pay our therapists their current rate or meet our expenses, let alone have a cushion for unanticipated problems or costs. I understood the need for the ACA and the good it would do for those without insurance, but it literally broke us as a business.

We thought about going back to being a self-paid-only center, but that idea didn't feel good. We knew families didn't have the money to keep up with the cost of this type of therapy. We discussed with the therapists the possibility of decreasing their pay and, as anyone would imagine, that was not well received. We looked at possibly becoming a non-profit so we could write grants for funding, but all of it felt like starting from scratch. We were exhausted and did not have it in us to try again.

After eight years in business, the decision was made to close the doors of Leap Beyond Therapy. We had to sell equipment, break leases, lay off employees, and pay all outstanding expenses. It was like nothing I had ever felt or dealt with before. I sobbed inconsolably for weeks.

Another therapy center bought most of the equipment, including the Therasuits, so they could offer this model of therapy at their center. The one owner said to the therapist, "Well, what do you think? This is going to be your baby to nurture!"

No! It wasn't her baby; it was my baby! My baby that I had nurtured and taken care of for eight years.

With the demise of Leap Beyond Therapy came the loss of contact with families, loss of friendship with my co-owner and therapists, and a loss of purpose for me. I didn't know what I was going to do moving forward. It was such a huge part of my life. To this day, I still miss my clients, families, and friends who were all part of Leap Beyond Therapy. I'm connected on social media with some of them, but not many, and the friendships and camaraderie are not the same.

Life can be weird. People come and go.

***

Here's a well-known poem. I'm sure you have seen or heard it before:

A REASON, A SEASON, OR A LIFETIME

People always come into your life for a reason, a season or a lifetime. When you figure out which it is, you know exactly what to do. When someone is in your life for a REASON, it is usually to meet a need you have expressed outwardly or inwardly. They have come to assist you through a difficulty, or to provide you with guidance and support, to aid you physically, emotionally, or even spiritually. They may seem like a godsend to you, and they are. They are there for a reason, you need them to be. Then, without any wrongdoing on your part or at an inconvenient time, this person will say or do something to bring the relationship to an end. Sometimes they die, sometimes they just walk away. Sometimes they act up or out and force you to take a stand. What we must realize is that our need has been met, our desire fulfilled; their work is done. The prayer you sent up has been answered and it is now time to move on. When people come into your life for a SEASON, it is because your turn has come to share, grow, or learn. They may bring you an experience of peace or make you laugh. They may teach you something you have never done. They usually give you an unbelievable amount of joy. Believe it! It is real! But, only for a season. And like Spring turns to Summer and Summer to Fall, the season eventually ends. LIFETIME relationships teach you a lifetime of lessons; those things you must build upon in order to have a solid emotional foundation. Your job is to accept the lesson, love the person/people (anyway); and put what you have learned to use in all other relationships and areas in your life. It is said that love is blind but friendship is clairvoyant.

—Author Unknown

* * *

The Universe at play. It knows what we need, when we need it, by who, and for how long.

It is not just relationships though. It can be challenges, hurdles, or even celebrations.

Teachers, early intervention specialists, and others came into my life for a "reason." They helped me to get information or things to help me on my journey. Once the grade was completed, or the equipment was purchased, they moved on.

Fellow families and friends who understand and experience this journey of special needs are "seasons." They bring joy, friendship, and lessons. But the season ends as we go different directions or part ways.

My parents, siblings, family, and my cerebral palsy, are a "lifetime." **They will all be with me until the end and will provide a lifetime of lessons.**

Can you look at your life and see reasons, seasons, and lifetimes with relationships, problems, or even blessings?

Follow Your Gut and Intuition

As a family, we never let Mason's disability deter us from activities, events, or doing things. We were a unit, a family of five. Sometimes we had to plan, sometimes we had to improvise, and sometimes we just had to make do. We just figured it out!

Even with our united front, Mason's disability did impact our family. In the excitement of getting ready for a family wedding, Mason would melt down. His crying, demanding, and screaming would sour the mood in our house in seconds.

Having to be "slow" at amusement parks or recreation centers because of Mason and his equipment became frustrating, especially for Leah and Quinn. They wanted to go, run, and play! But they would patiently wait as we all corralled into the place with the wheelchair, canes, and oftentimes, a hesitant child.

As the years accumulated, it was clear Leah and Quinn had strong feelings about Mason's disability. Not the disability itself, but the impact it had on the family. Especially the impact it had on me. Leah and Quinn didn't like how much work was required of me to do things for Mason. They could see and feel my exhaustion, and sometimes despair.

As much as I pushed Mason to get stronger, be independent, and do for himself, I still had to do a lot for him.

When Mason would have meltdowns, Leah and Quinn would get aggravated. "Mason is at it again" was written all over their faces. They saw his behaviors as manipulative and controlling.

Don't get me wrong. Leah and Quinn LOVE Mason! They would do anything for him. They make time for him, share laughs, and have fun with Mason all the time. But they weren't wrong in some of their thinking. Mason's disability impacted our family. They saw discrimination, they saw the work, and they saw the hurt. They empathized with those directly affected by it—their parents, Mason, other children and families—and they still do.

They also gained knowledge, compassion, and numerous other characteristics that have helped them through life and developed who they are. Big-hearted. Leaders. Goal-oriented. Inclusive. Hard-working. Out-of-the-box thinkers. Funny. Empathetic. Accepting. Loving. Non-judgmental. Creative. Bold. Go-Getters. Energetic. Smart. Life-long learners. Seekers. Doers. Advocates. Information-seekers. The list goes on and on.

Could these characteristics be genetic? Sure. But I believe they have been taught through growing up in our family and being challenged with all the things that transpire and evolve from having a disability. Just like alcoholism, disability affects not only the person who has it but also those who surround that person.

***

My friend, Annie, had gotten movie tickets at work for Evan Almighty. She and I decided to take the kids to a movie.

The movie theatre had the cinemas upstairs from the main entrance. Of course, the elevator wasn't in a convenient place. Since Mason was walking with his canes and I didn't want to him truck to the other side of the place to get in the elevator and then have to truck back, I decided we could get him on the escalator. Mason was scared of the escalator, but as always, he was willing to give it a try. With a lot of encouragement and simple "step now" instructions, we made our way up the escalator. Mason was giddy, and so proud of himself. We got off with a little bit of stumble, but no one was on the floor, so that was good.

After the movie was over, Annie and I made our way down the escalator. Mason was with Leah and Quinn. At the bottom of the escalator, we looked up to see Mason hesitant and not really wanting to get on. With a lot of encouragement and persistence, Leah finally convinced Mason it was going to be okay and that she would tell him when to step. She took his canes, held his hand, got on the escalator in front of him and said, "step now." The thing with spastic diplegia cerebral palsy is you become stiff, especially when under stress. Mason's stiff step caused him to hang off the step, and he was struggling. Leah was trying to help him, but she got off balance, and whoosh, down they went! Leah on the bottom, and Mason on top. Somehow Quinn, who was behind Mason, ended up also falling into the jumbled pile.

It was like people bowling balls bumping down each step! I'm not going to lie, it looked hilarious, and we were all laughing . . . until the bottom.

You see, an escalator doesn't stop, unless you hit the emergency stop button, which we were not bright enough to do at the time. So, as the children laid in a heap on the comb plate at the bottom of the escalator, the "teeth" were "chewing" their skin, and the continued motion was causing a burn. Leah was on the bottom of the pile, and with the boys on top of her, she was unable to get up. No one could get up. Annie and I grabbed Quinn, then Mason, and pulled them off. After getting the boys off Leah, she was able to stand up.

Scrapes, burns, and blood covered all three of their arms, legs, knees, and elbows. It was a wonder no one was seriously hurt. After everyone was safe and retrieved, we realized how bad and serious this escapade could have really been.

To say Mason was afraid and not willing to try escalators again would be an understatement!

***

I don't think Leah and Quinn really have a true understanding of how difficult it can be to live with cerebral palsy. Part of me is appreciative of the fact that they see me as a capable human—"get your own damn soda out of the fridge"—but the other part of me gets upset because honestly, I don't want to have to ask for help. I would much rather get it myself! I hate that I need my mom to do and help with so many things. I also must pick and choose what things to do, and when, to conserve energy.

As far as events like weddings, amusement parks, and other activities, an overwhelming anxiety comes over me when I go to unknown venues, am around large amounts of people, or have limited control in situations.

I don't like to admit these things, and I don't think people always understand the depth of my anxiety around them. Growing up, I often made excuses about not feeling well to get out of going. Fear was encompassing me and causing me to not want to try, and I wanted to isolate.

Hey, I wasn't trying to pee on anyone's parade, I was just trying to survive. But I can see how they don't see it that way.

I love Leah and Quinn! They are my people. I can't lie and say I'm not jealous of the relationship Leah and Quinn share and wish I could be a larger part of that. But I am who I am. I know they love me. I know they want the best for me, as I do for them. We are just different.

***

Escalators! They are my nemesis! I despise them. They have provoked a fear in me for the rest of my life.

***

As a result of our questioning and uncertainty at times with our local hospital about Mason's care and treatment, we found a cerebral palsy center in Missouri and began following their team. The head neurologist of the center had cerebral palsy herself, so not only had she studied it, she also lived it. She became a lifelong resource for us. Although she is no longer in Missouri (she opened her own practice), we still travel out of state to see her and check in. Mason was three years old at his first visit with her and at the time of writing this book he is twenty-five. We have the utmost respect for her and are thankful we found her.

Even though we sought other opinions through referrals, travels, and research, we remained with our local hospital. We went to appointments because their opinions and recommendations were also important. It's all about getting the information you can at the time and making the best decision with that information.

***

I still see that same neurologist twenty-two years later!

I wish I had the right words to express my gratitude to my parents for going above and beyond. I don't think there are many parents who would do as much research as my parents did, question medical professionals, and even not agree with them to the point that they pursued other options, many of which ended up being out of state.

I know if my parents had not followed their gut or fought against the grain, I would not be as functional and independent as I am today. I know this drive was a big part of my story.

Even when I think their determination changed from "fixing it" to acceptance, it still pressed them to get me physically as far as they could.

You need to listen to yourself. Your gut is smarter than your head. If you feel something within yourself, know it is right!

Kudos to my parents for following their gut and intuition.

Depression and Anxiety, Meet Cerebral Palsy

The school years.

Elementary school excelled at making accommodations for Mason and including him in activities. He had terrific teachers and paraprofessionals. The staff in the building did what we did—they just made it work!

Elementary school was where Individualized Educational Plan (IEP) meetings became a big thing.

IEPs. Sigh.

The meetings consisted of forms with check marks in boxes, basically denoting the students' limitations and highlighting all the things they cannot do.

A constant reminder on paper.

We lived this. Every. Single. Day.

Just like our experience with the medical field: "Here's the options, fit into them."

"But, there must be other options. Other ways."

These meetings and forms clashed with our desires. Rick and I never left an IEP feeling great. It just felt like we were drafting a paper to cover someone's ass versus helping our son. But we did what all parents had to do and just went with it.

Despite the deflating meetings, Mason felt love and support throughout elementary school because of the staff. They were always kind and great with him. However, as with everything, the elementary years brought various events that have stayed with me.

I will never forget several incidents in the first grade.

The first incident was at an open house. A mother approached me and told me her son, Atticus, adored Mason and that they had been playing on the playground together. She went on to explain she and Atticus had been talking about Mason for weeks and she had no idea Mason had a handicap from the conversations they had.

She continued. "When I asked Atticus why he didn't tell me Mason had a handicap, he responded 'What's the big deal, Mom?'"

The second incident was Mason had just gotten new DAFOs (dynamic ankle foot orthotics), and they were bothering his feet. His paraprofessional asked the school secretary to call me and see if I could bring up his old ones for the rest of the day. That was not a problem. I drove up to the school, went into the office, and asked if I could take Mason his braces. The secretary called down to the classroom to let the teacher know I was there and see if it was okay for me to come down. She adamantly refused. She explained to the secretary that there are procedures for parents volunteering and that I had not followed that procedure. The secretary assured her I wasn't volunteering, I just wanted to help with Mason's braces. The teacher told her Mason's paraprofessional would figure it out.

I was furious! This was the most ridiculous thing I had ever heard of! I went to the principal, who backed the teacher up.

WTF!

I began asking questions like, "What is the teacher hiding that I'm not supposed to see?" "Do you realize you guys called me to come up here?" My daughter attended the school for years, and I never had any issues with anything. Today they were acting so weird about it, to the point I wanted to sign Mason out and not bring him back. It was like a prison denying visitors. It did not sit well with me.

Later, I did ask the teacher about it, and she said, "Policies are policies. The policy states parents must give 24-hour notice to visit classrooms."

Obviously, this has remained a thorn in my side!

***

It was second grade when I received a phone call.

"Mrs. Bailey? Hi, my name is Krista and I am the mother of Ryan who is in Mason's class. I wanted to call you because Ryan is having a birthday party at the local rollarena and he is adamant about having Mason come."

"Oh my gosh, how nice! I'm sure Mason would love that!" My mind quickly went to thinking how I could help Mason skate. I thought I could push him in his wheelchair with me skating behind.

Krista went on to say how she explained to Ryan that Mason may not be able to skate and said Ryan's response was, "I don't care, I just want him there. He's my friend!"

I told Krista she must be extremely proud of the son she was raising. "Mason would love to come, and there's always food and video games if we can't get him on the skating floor."

Mason was so excited when I told him about Ryan inviting him to his party! Mason exclaimed, "Yeah, me and Ryan are really good friends."

My heart swelled with these words. First true friend, Nolan. And now, Ryan!

***

In third grade, the school planned a field trip to the zoo. Permission slips were sent home. In the upcoming days I asked Mason how they were going to get his wheelchair there.

"I have no idea."

I sent an email inquiring how they were going to accommodate Mason's wheelchair, as the zoo was simply too big for him to walk. The response I got was not what I expected. Basically, they had not thought about it. They thanked me as they realized they would need to make a request for the handicap-accessible bus so Mason could attend.

I explained the accessible bus really wasn't warranted and that Mason would like to ride with his peers. I went on to say his wheelchair could easily be folded and placed on the bus for when he got to the zoo.

They declared this a "safety issue," as the chair would not be secured and could potentially be a danger for the students or driver.

Seriously? My response was, "Can't we just put the chair in a seat and secure it with strapping?"

Which is what they ended up doing.

I was so baffled. Baffled by the mere fact that they had not even thought of how to accommodate Mason for the field trip. Baffled that they immediately wanted to separate him from the class. Baffled because I knew in the multitude of years the school had run, they had to accommodate a student with a wheelchair before. But here we were, trying to help them help my son be included and have what he needed.

When this incident occurred, I was discussing it with other "club" parents. I remember their response: "Just wait for Camp Kern."

It was well known and talked about among fellow parents that students who have special needs were not particularly welcome to attend the annual fifth grade Camp Kern adventure. I heard things like. "Johnnie, who has Down syndrome, isn't going because there will not be air conditioning," "Susie, who uses a wheelchair is not going because paths aren't accessible," "Cleo, who has autism, would not be able to be 'contained' within the cabin," and "Trish would get scared at night, so it is probably best that she not attend." It was weird. Obviously, students who have special needs have special needs, but it was as if the staff was trying to convince the students and parents it wasn't in the best interest for the child to even try to attend.

So, after hearing this and experiencing the turmoil with the zoo field trip, I started to jokingly say to the elementary school principal, "I'm preparing you. Mason wants to and plans to attend Camp Kern in the fifth grade."

She would giggle and respond, "Okay." I did this a multitude of times each year for two years.

It was also in third grade that I picked Mason up from school only to find him in full-blown tears. Through his sobbing, he explained one of the students had invited everyone from the class to his birthday party except him. I consoled him and tried to tell him I bet it wasn't true that everyone was invited.

He said, "Oh yeah they are, Mom. The person having the party said so and the class was talking about it and how I wasn't invited."

What? What? What? C'mon, people. Can we just be kind?

The party was going to be held at an indoor trampoline park, and since Mason couldn't jump, he wasn't invited. The parent of the child who was having the party made sure to bring this to my attention one afternoon as I was dropping off baked goods for a bake sale the school was having.

"Mrs. Bailey, I wanted to let you know why Mason wasn't invited to my son's birthday party. You see, it is at a trampoline park, and since Mason cannot jump, I told my son we would take him separately to a movie sometime."

I nodded and said okay as I didn't have it in me to explain the hurt she had caused. The invite to a movie never happened.

***

As Mason entered fifth grade, he started experiencing intense pain because his muscles were not stretching as his bones grew. Medical professionals in our area recommended muscle lengthening, which seemed scary and premature since Mason was still so young. I asked the local orthopedic surgeon if he corrected the tendon or lengthened the muscle, would Mason be able to return to walking, and if so, when.

He answered, "I'm not sure. It depends on how his legs respond to the neurological input from his brain once I fix them."

Uh, what? I took his response to mean, "I can fix the orthopedic part, but I don't know how the cerebral palsy pieces will respond." That was not okay. We needed someone who understood both! We began to research again and found an orthopedic surgeon on the East Coast who performed percutaneous muscle lengthening. The procedure did not cut into the muscle at all; the surgeon would merely poke tiny holes in the muscle so it was pliable enough to stretch. The stretch was then obtained through casting for several weeks.

We traveled out east several times throughout Mason's growth spurts to have this procedure done. Each time we went it was frowned upon by our local medical team. They did not believe in the surgeon and felt the medical research was not there.

Well, I remembered hearing that before.

Don't get me wrong. The staff at our local hospital is incredible, and they do amazing work! Mason, Rick, and I have close relationships with them. We utilized their physical therapies and saw their doctors, but we always considered all the information, local and non-local. We had to do what we felt was best, regardless of others' opinions, even our hometown medical team.

As Mason's pain increased, we didn't feel we could wait for additional research to be done. We had a growing child, one we wanted to succeed. We wanted him to become as functional as possible. This less invasive procedure, called PERCs (selective percutaneous myofascial lengthening), seemed to be the best option. Again, this doesn't mean our local medical team was wrong or not good therapists or doctors. For our family, and at that time, we just didn't feel they were the route we wanted to take.

***

The first surgery went well, and Mason recovered fairly quickly. After PERCs, the patient is casted to allow the muscles to stretch from the procedure. The casts gave Mason stability and discomfort was minimal.

We had a one-month post-op visit in New Jersey. We were at the airport awaiting boarding to come home. Multiple upon multiple times, I asked Mason if he needed to use the restroom before we boarded. I knew he had airplane anxiety and on top of that the thought of trying to get Mason down the aisle to the small restroom seemed daunting. Mason assured me he did not need to use the bathroom.

"Flight three two four nine now boarding."

"Mom, I need to go to the bathroom."

"Mason. Seriously?"

"Yes, it just hit me."

I transferred him over to his wheelchair from the lobby chair and busted a move to the ladies' restroom, which had a line. Once, the handicap stall opened we made a mad dash in. I hurriedly transferred him over to the toilet, helping him get his pants down and making sure all things were out of aim's way. He immediately peed. As I went to get him back in his wheelchair, he said "Wait, I think I have to poop."

"Mason, we don't have time for this. We are going to miss our flight."

"Mom, I can't help it. I have to go."

Anxiously I waited, paced the stall area, and kept watching Mason. Mason did not seem to be concentrating that much on going to the bathroom.

"Mason, do you really have to go?"

"Yes, Mom."

Tapping my foot and wondering what I was going to do if we missed the plane, I finally told Mason, "You are going to have to go poop on the plane. We don't have time."

He started throwing a fit. A fit that was obviously not about pooping, but about getting on the plane! He was hoping to miss the flight.

I hear "Last call for Flight three two four nine."

I grabbed Mason and quickly placed him in the wheelchair with him yelling and carrying on. As we scurried out of the stall, everyone was staring, and my soul was telling me, "Someone is going to be calling 241-KIDS on me." By that time, not only was I panicking, but I was also pissed. We made it to the door as the flight attendant was releasing the catch to close it. I was relieved but my heart remained pounding for some time as we got into the air.

WTH Mason Bailey!

* * *

After the distraction of Mason's need for surgery was over, I began the process of asking for meetings for Mason to be able to attend Camp Kern in the spring. Everyone obliged and faithfully wrote down the jargon needed on Mason's IEP.

Camp Kern had high school student volunteers who oversaw the students in cabins and helped with activities. I mandated that Mason's high school student meet him beforehand to be sure they were comfortable with him and his needs. Everything seemed to be going smoothly, so much so I was baffled that previous families had problems with getting Camp Kern accommodations.

Camp took place in March. It was in the month of February that Mason came home distraught. The teacher who headed Camp Kern was also a teacher he had in class. Mason explained to me that the teacher kept asking him how he was going to get around at camp. I told Mason to tell her we would figure it out.

Then one day, Mason was sitting at his desk, and the teacher bent down and whispered in Mason's ear, "What are you going to do when the Muskrat rifle gets fired off at Camp Kern?"

She was referring to Mason's extreme startle reflex. She was aware of his aversion to loud noises as his IEP had him escorted out prior to fire drills. When Mason came home and told me this, I called a meeting. It now had become blatantly obvious that it was not the school not wanting certain students to attend camp, but the teacher who was head of the camp! You can guarantee I made this known in the impromptu meeting, describing the teacher's behaviors. The school backed the teacher, stating she was just concerned, and that safety is the district's number one priority for all students. I started questioning my persistence in getting him to go and began thinking maybe he shouldn't.

Mason wanted to go. Mason did not understand or see any reason why he couldn't go. So, what did I do? I called Camp Kern and asked if I could tour the facility. I asked if they would be willing to show me their accommodations and the different activities they did with the students.

"Absolutely, Mrs. Bailey. When would you like to come?"

Camp Kern was a beautiful facility. They showed me a housing unit where students could stay if they needed air conditioning. They suggested Mason stay in this area, not due to the air conditioning, but because it had a handicap accessible shower. We looked at trails they used, and I asked if they would allow Mason to bring his accessible bike as it would probably be much easier on the trails than his wheelchair.

"Sure!"

They asked if Mason had any dietary restrictions or medical needs to be addressed.

I said, "No."

I asked about the shooting of the Muskrat, and if it was something they did as part of a ceremony. They responded it was and offered Mason the option of using headphones or being assisted back to the house when it was shot off.

Well, look at that, Momma Bear was right. He could and would be attending Camp Kern! After meeting with the camp staff and touring the facility, I called another school meeting to share what I was told and saw. I asked Mason's teacher to come to the meeting. I explained Mason would be staying in the house with access to the handicap-accessible shower. I continued with that he would be bringing his bike, and that he needed to be asked if he wanted headphones or to be removed from the area for the shooting of the Muskrat.

The teacher sputtered, "Bike? How are we going to get his bike there? That is a large bike."

I assured her I was more than happy to drop it off at camp prior to their arrival.

She continued. "Who is going to be responsible for getting Mason on and off the bike? He is entirely too big to lift."

I assured her Mason could handle getting on and off himself, that someone would merely need to hold his canes for him. You could tell by the look on her face she knew I wasn't playing.

Mason had the absolute best time at Camp Kern! He had an incredible student volunteer and he said they stayed up late at night talking and laughing. He said at first they were leery about the bike thing, but once he got on and was able to ride it, they were thrilled. He said there was one small incline that required the student volunteer to give him a push so he could make it up, but other than that, he was golden.

***

Sixth grade graduation was held in the gym. They had set up a stage for the students to walk up the stairs to and sit on the bleachers. There were chairs on the floor for the families of the students graduating.

Yep, you guessed it! No one had thought about how Mason would get on the stage. The stairs they had did not have a railing. When I inquired, their solution was Mason could use his wheelchair and sit in front of the stage. ERGH!

"No, I'm sorry but that is not going to work. I am not going to have Mason excluded from his classmates and be a focal point in a wheelchair."

Miraculously, they found stairs with railings on each side that could be rolled up to the stage. Arrangements were made for Mason's paraprofessional to take his canes so he could go up the steps, then hand them back to him so he could go sit on the bleachers.

I don't know how to explain it, but asking about things for Mason in his elementary years started the mother feelings of "we're a problem." My inquiries and requests were never well-received. Everyone was nice about it, but there was a feeling of giving them extra work, annoyance, and just being "that" parent.

Honestly, I didn't think I was asking for too much.

***

Kindergarten through sixth grade were my best school years, yet I still housed a reservation about going. The staff was so kind, loving and accommodating to me. We shared laughs, good times, and they helped me tremendously.

All my memories are with my teachers, paraprofessionals, and other staff. I believe that is because I am an old soul. I can relate to adults, and they can relate to me.

It was in elementary school that it permeated every cell of my being that I was not accepted among peers. Sure, the kids were nice, but they held their distance. Interactions were when necessary and usually with skepticism. There were a few exceptional friendships, such as Ryan, Atticus, Danni, Neil and Jenica, but for the most part I relished in adult interactions.

I got reminded on a regular basis that I was not accepted by peers when I did not get invited to birthday parties or after-school events with them. IEP meetings were all about things I could not do, not the things I could do.

***

In elementary school, I had to undergo several orthopedic surgeries. My mobility cycled through cane, walker, and wheelchair. As soon as I would get back to where I was, another procedure would be scheduled to address another area causing me pain.

I could see and feel a difference with my out-of-state doctors. They made me feel more comfortable, and they definitely made my parents feel more comfortable with their surgical options.

***

When I lack control, my anxiety soars. I think when you have a body you have minimal control over, it increases your desire to have control over things you can. Surgeries involve a major lack of control, leading to tremendous fear. I know this is probably true for everyone, but my feelings were over the top! As a result, I would grab hold of anything I could control.

By far, my biggest grab was always at the airport when we flew. I would make one of my parents take me to the bathroom and I'd delay as long as I could. There were some pretty good arguments trying to get me on and off planes. I still carry anxiety about flying, and I think it's because every trip I've flown for has been for a medical reason, whether an appointment or surgery. I mean, sometimes we would do fun things before or after appointments in the place we traveled, but first and foremost, we were there for medical reasons.

***

Camp Kern was a highlight for me. I could not wait to be able to go away to camp, away from home, in a cabin! My excitement dwindled quickly though as I saw the conflicts between my mom and school when they discussed me going.

As years went on, I was soaking in the not belonging, not being accepted, all based on my body being disabled. It was in those years that I began to sense I needed to prove myself to others. I needed to prove my "disabled" body could do the things others thought it couldn't. I would push myself as hard as I could to achieve all the things that people thought I couldn't.

I started trying to be and do what I thought other people wanted from me. I was doing exactly what humans should not do—transforming into what other people want them to be or do.

***

Elementary school had its challenges, but it got worse in middle school.

Let me begin with the fire drill. Mason had an extreme fear of fire drills. He watched for, anguished about, and even counted days to try and figure out when the monthly fire drill would be. The anxiety of these drills caused him to fake being sick and have massive meltdowns and angry outbursts to the point that he could not function. This had been an issue from the beginning of school.

In elementary school, and even preschool, it was in his IEP that he should be told and taken out of the classroom prior to the fire drill. But in middle school, they felt Mason should be able to "handle" the fire drills. They felt he should not have to be told ahead of time. They said it wasn't an accurate drill if he was aware of it. In the middle school building, unlike the elementary school building, there were stairs (or an elevator, which you cannot use during a fire drill), so this compounded Mason's anxiety.

For years we tried (us as parents, and the school personnel) to figure out the fear of fire drills. Was it the loud, unexpected sound that startled him? Was it the fear of being trampled? Was it the fear of being left? Was it the fire department arriving with lights and sirens? Whatever the reason, Mason was NOT having it! He was not backing down on his fire drill stance. It got to the point that we either produced a solid plan or he was not going to school.

I know what you're thinking: "You're the parent, just take him to school!"

Well, sure, we tried that too.

The melting down, frantic, inconsolable, screaming child was welcomed in the building for about a hot second, then the school personnel was not having it either. I mean, seriously, if I could have dropped him off and left, I would have been all about it.

One day, the middle school principal experienced firsthand Mason's terrified reaction to not knowing about fire drills. I brought him into school in full meltdown. The principal assured him there would not be a fire drill that day. Mason wanted to know when. A plan was finally put in place for Mason to be informed ahead of time about the drills and escorted out before the bell rang. This plan had to be followed, because if you broke Mason's trust, you broke Mason's trust. He didn't, and still doesn't, give you three strikes before you're out. You get one try, so you better get it right.

The staff was so accommodating after that. It became a secret mission for them and Mason. He would be notified in confidence and covertly led out of the building before the alarm sounded.

Phew! One huge hurdle cleared. Thank goodness!

The second hurdle in middle school came when Mason had surgery in seventh grade. It was a huge surgery. His muscles were so tight they were pulling on the bones and "bowing" his legs. The surgery, done in Missouri, was a derotation of his femur and re-alignment of his tibia and fibula. He was supposed to be inpatient for several days. However, after the first twenty-four hours of staff going in and out all day and night, his IV beeping, O2 sat probe chirping, social workers inquiring about things, and therapists wanting to work with him, Mason's anxiety (and Rick's and mine) was through the roof. Since Mason's pain seem to be controlled, we asked if we could be discharged early. The physician did not have a problem with that, so he wrote the order.

Mason was out of school for a few months after the surgery. When he went back to school, he needed a wheelchair. Up to this point, Mason had handed his canes to the bus driver, walked up the steps, and took a seat. I'm not going to lie, there were a few bus drivers that did not like this, but it didn't take Mason long to win their hearts with his conversation and personality. After he did that, they didn't think about his canes for a second. One bus driver in particular, who was filling in for another driver, questioned his canes immediately. She didn't want to take them from him. She glared at him and me and questioned why he was on her bus. She had dark short hair, wore a beret, and seemed to carry a heavy chip on her shoulder. Mason told me he didn't know why Tamara was so mean and asked me what he should do.

"Mason, do what you always do—kill her with kindness."

It hadn't even been a full week when I went out to the end of the driveway and found Mason and Tamara laughing as he was exiting the bus.

I said to Mason, "What was that all about?"

"Let's just say I broke her. We were talking about McDonald's and how we both like the Quarter Pounder with cheese."

After that, friends, you could tell Tamara looked forward to Mason getting on and off her bus.

After surgery Mason required the handicap-accessible bus. Tamara, who once wanted Mason off her bus, was now disappointed he wasn't going to be riding with her. We lived on the street between the elementary school and high school; it cut through the township, taking you from one side to the other. The road was thirty-five miles per hour and had slight curves. It was honestly a quiet street for the most part, quieter than you might think, EXCEPT when school was starting or ending. During those times, we got all the traffic from the students, parents, and staff.

When the wheelchair-accessible bus stopped at our driveway, the bus driver would get out, come around to the back of the bus, lower the loading gate (which is a slow process), get Mason and his chair on the gate, secure him, press the button to raise the gate (just as slow), wheel him into the bus, secure his chair to the platform so he was safe during the ride, secure the gate so it doesn't fall down during the drive, walk to the front of the bus, turn the stop lights off, put it in gear, and begin the drive to school.

Well . . . like I said, this was not a fast process. And, as it was taking place, you had the students, parents, employees, and randoms coming down the street and getting stopped by the bus. Cars backed up.

I don't even know if it had been a full week of Mason using the accessible bus when I received a call from the principal. He wanted to talk to me about the "bus situation." I didn't think anything about it. I was thinking maybe they would need to change drivers, or there was a maintenance issue or something.

No, he wanted to talk to me about the "unsafe" situation caused by the bus loading and unloading Mason before and after school.

"Unsafe?" I repeated.

"Yes, I am sure you have noticed that during the process of getting Mason on and off the bus that traffic is getting backed up on both sides of the street?"

I was amused and inquired, "How is this unsafe?"

He began to hem haw around, saying the cars are lined up for miles. The process was causing students to be delayed getting to and from school, and we needed to address the issue.

I don't know why or how, and maybe you get it within yourself too, but sometimes a "This is BS and is not MY problem" feeling fills my body. This was one of those times.

"With all due respect sir, this 'bus situation' is not an unsafe situation. It is merely an inconvenience for those traveling at the same time. The traffic being stopped does not make anyone unsafe. I am sorry my son had to have surgery due to his disability. I am sorry we require the wheelchair-accessible bus. I am sorry the driver must follow a certain procedure to load and unload my son, but there is nothing unsafe about this!"

"Mrs. Bailey, we have been receiving a multitude of calls from drivers regarding this 'situation,' and I think we need to address it."

"I suggest you address it by telling the drivers they have three choices: They can leave at a different time, either earlier or later than they are currently; they can drive a different way to avoid our street, there are other ways to get to their destination; or they can develop patience and gratitude that our situation is merely an inconvenience for them and not a lifelong commitment."

I wasn't having it! As a matter of fact, I was struggling to regulate my anger due to the lack of understanding and empathy.

***

It was a Saturday. We were invited to a wedding aboard a riverboat and we were all looking forward to it. Before the ceremony we enjoyed the day as a family; we swam, played pool volleyball, and had lunch. Later in the afternoon, we began getting dressed for the wedding.

I dressed Mason in tan chinos and a button-down shirt. He looked handsome. He wasn't fighting me, but you could tell he wasn't liking it. I went into my bedroom to get dressed. As I was pulling my dress over my head, Mason and Rick got into a heated discussion. Rick was trying to get Mason to allow him to put his shoes on. Mason was fighting him and not wanting to wear the shoes.

I swept in to defuse the argument. "It's fine. Mason can wear his gym shoes. It's fine."

You could tell Rick was disgusted. He doesn't believe in rewarding bad behavior, and while I agree, I also don't like to deal with the ramifications of Tornado Mason. I know it's one of my mothering flaws in raising him, but I chose my battles. Believe me, there were a lot of battles to choose! This flaw was also a bone of contention with Mason's siblings. Leah and Quinn hated when Mason won, and they hated when it affected me, my plans, or the family plans.

Even though I approved the gym shoes, Mason went into "I'm not going to this stupid wedding" mode.

Rick went into angry power mode. "Oh yes you are! You don't have a choice, young man."

Leah and Quinn exchanged the "here we go" look.

Our looking forward to going to the riverboat wedding turned into "should we even go?" A full-blown crying, screaming meltdown Mason-style commenced. Somehow, through the yelling, fighting, and disgust, we ended up getting to the wedding. However, our excitement and anticipation was diminished to "we just need to get through this."

The wedding was beautiful! The weather was perfect. The dinner reception was delicious. We ended up sitting at a table with the groom's brother and his friend. His friend had cerebral palsy too, and our family, including Mason, shared a night of friendship and laughs. It ended up being an extremely enjoyable time, but it was hectic getting to that point.

***

I'm telling you right now—me and fire drills were NOT happening! I refused to stay in the building during them in elementary school and I continued to refuse through high school. I may have been able to push myself through some things, but never a fire drill. I don't know if it was from my vacuum cleaner fear, the unexpected loud alarm, or the fact I felt I could be trampled, but I was not going to be part of an active fire drill. No way, no how.

I had the ears of an elephant! Those teachers would talk amongst themselves, holding their folders up so I couldn't see their lips, but I heard them discussing the fire drill and when it was going to happen. I couldn't concentrate or think about anything else until I knew there was a plan for me. It took two well-played-out drills for me to trust that the staff was going to stick to the plan.

***

If I had to use my chair, I had to use it. And me using my chair meant the bus would have to stop traffic. Sorry guys! I was all about the buttons the driver had to press to initiate the red flashing stop lights and to lower the ramp. I concentrated on him securing the tie-downs to my chair and putting the bus in gear. I loved the process of getting me onto the bus. My mom and the principal discussing the situation was comical to me. Just another day in the Mason Bailey life, causing conflict, rife, and dismay.

***

Our best family memories were going to the Kentucky farm or trails to ride ATVs. Mason had grown up on his battery-operated toys, then graduated to ATVs, thus exposing Leah and Quinn to them as well. It was a family event where everyone enjoyed themselves, and there wasn't a disability to be seen. Riding was when Mason felt most free. We kept to the easy trails, wore helmets, and of course found all the mud puddles possible. There was something peaceful and soothing about being together in nature among trees, dust, a cool breeze, and mud!

I will never forget the check-in appointments with the physical medicine rehabilitation doctor in Mason's adolescent years. He was a very sincere and kind physician. He was hesitant about some of our treatment choices, which he voiced at our scheduled visits. I appreciated his honesty, and we adored him. He always reprimanded us for allowing Mason to ride ATVs. He would tell us stories of patients he saw due to having accidents on ATVs. Mason would joke, "I already have brain damage, so if I wreck, a little more damage won't hurt." The doctor did not find his remark amusing. It was an off-color response, I admit.

At a check-in appointment many years after Mason had recovered from his SDR and PERCs, the physician said, "Mason is doing really well. Mom, you've done a good job!"

I took that as, "You made the right decisions for him, despite me not agreeing with you at times."

**

Middle school brought Mason being sent to special education classrooms. As the weeks went on, Mason began feeling isolated from his friends. He was in a class where they were teaching life skills. These life skills were folding pizza boxes, watering plastic flowers, and wrapping up silverware in napkins. Mason adamantly began to put his foot down, saying he wasn't going back to that class.

I sent an email inquiring more about the class and if there were other class options for Mason to attend. The very next day, Mason walked into "I got your mom's email this morning. What's going on, Mason?" He came home and told me not to send emails anymore because they were not well-received. This whole situation with the class and email resulted in a meeting being called. The meeting was to explain that Mason's perspective and interpretation of the class were not correct.

Did they just say to Mason that he wasn't correct in his thinking? Yup, they sure did!

Mason said, "Whether I am correct or not, I am not taking that class anymore."

Trying to take advantage of the lull before the storm, I interjected. "Are there other life skills that maybe Mason could participate in, such as a keyboard class?"

The occupational therapist at the table felt strongly that Mason would not be able to learn how to use a keyboard with his disability.

Again, I suggested, "He may not be able to use it proficiently like you and me with the standard finger strikes, but maybe continual practice would lead to a pace that would be faster than his ability to write."

The meeting concluded with us getting Mason out of the life skills class and into a small group math class.

On the car ride home, Mason said, "Did she say she didn't think I could learn how to type?"

Rick answered, "Yes, I think that is what she said."

Mason muttered, "Do people not know I can do whatever I want to do?"

***

My friends from elementary school were no longer accessible to me, as I was placed in special education classes. The school work they had me doing was humiliating. I was instructed in one class to water plastic flowers and roll crayons up in napkins. I remember them saying, "These are actual things restaurants pay people to do. These things are for employment."

I'm telling you right now, if anyone ever pays someone for watering plastic flowers, they need to be evaluated!

When I told my mom about my day and what they were having me do, she would immediately email the staff. Her emails were never malicious, she was merely trying to make things better for me. It got to the point though where I had to tell her to quit emailing the staff because I would walk in and the first thing they would say is, "I got another email from your mom today."

Mom was furious they were confronting me about her emails.

***

It was in middle school that we identified there was a "gap" in Mason's educational progress. Mason's gap was increasing, and we were not seeing any progress or plan being put in place to close it. With a little help from good ole Google, we discovered the middle school was identified as having difficulty "closing the gap" on the state's report card. The school had a D in this area.

It was then we began to have Mason privately tested. Yes, the district should have paid for it, but you choose your battles. We also requested the school to do testing so the assessments and evaluations could be compared. We learned about researched-based reading. Just like the local hospital wanted evidence-based research to prove authenticity, the education system did the same. School districts were supposed to implement a research-based (proven) reading program for struggling students.

That was not happening.

At an open house, Rick and I went into Mason's reading class. The instructor explained her course, and the way she taught. She was very kind. At one point, she asked if there were any questions. I raised my hand and asked, "Do you use any research-based instruction?"

She replied, "Pieces from different models."

Rick and I were at a loss on how to handle Mason's education and make sure he was getting the instruction and accommodations he needed to be successful. We ended up hiring an inclusion advocate. This advocate was phenomenal and would attend IEP meetings with us. She helped us navigate the legalities of the system. We needed to know what they were required to do, not do, provide, not provide, and how to verbalize things so Mason's academic needs could be met.

At one point, she encouraged us to make a written request to the school about any conversations regarding Mason and his education. It was because of this request that we learned about the email sent from Mason's reading teacher to the principal that said, "Mason's parents attended my open house, and when I opened it up for questions, they 'started in on me.'"

I was flabbergasted! I merely asked one question. I wanted to "start in on her" after reading that! After that email was sent and we hired the inclusion advocate, we were informed that Rick and I could not talk to or be in a room with a staff member without someone else from the school present, for everyone's protection.

Geez Louise!

Our relationship at the middle school became contentious for both sides. Meetings became heated, intense, and miserable. Regardless of how well we prepared, knew what was required by law, and tried to educate the team around the table, there was never any agreement. It was offense and defense on the field! The more we pushed, the harder they defended.

***

The relationship between my parents and the school district became tenuous.

This disgruntled relationship began to take a bigger toll on me. Staff never said it, and it may not have been seen, but man, I felt it! I can always feel the energy of a person or a room. I felt the anger within staff. I felt their disgust. I knew they felt like they were walking on eggshells around us.

I did not care. I was done!

***

Because the school and the district refused to put research-based reading in place for Mason, we pulled him out of school in the morning to attend a private researched-based reading center.

Full circle, friends. First we were fighting the hospital because they wanted research-based therapy models and we didn't. Now we were fighting to get research-based reading and weren't receiving it. The district was responsible for providing this service and should have paid for independent facilities or teachers if they couldn't provide it, but they refused. They said their assessments and evaluations were different from our private ones and they did not believe or see the same things. They were adamant the classes Mason was in were in his best interest and they were complying legally. It was the classic "fit into our box because we don't have anywhere else to put him."

Then the district threatened that if Mason didn't come to school and we continued to take him out for the private reading program it could be considered truancy, and there could be ramifications. It became a war. They were as determined as we were, and there didn't seem to be any way to meet in the middle.

We decided to hire an attorney. He assured us the school would not be able to do anything if we chose to send Mason to a private reading center, so that's what we decided to do. I would take Mason to the center first thing in the morning, then take him to school for his other classes. The first day we pulled up to the middle school after the reading program, there was a sheriff's car sitting out front. Mason and I were certain they were waiting to arrest him for truancy. I pulled out my cell phone and called the attorney.

The attorney's response? "Take your phone and record everything that happens and we'll take it to the media!"

Oh great! Just what I wanted to be involved in—a media story about fighting to get what my son needed and legally deserved! Mason and I were scared, but we went in. I signed him into school and he went to class. No one was arrested, and we never found out why the sheriff was there.

The heated disagreements between us and the school and district continued. We ended up asking our private evaluators to come to the school, share results, and have discussions. That IEP meeting consisted of twenty-four people around a huge circular table, including our attorney, the district attorney, our private evaluators, district evaluators, teachers, advocates, and us. After an hour-and-a-half, the meeting ended with no resolution. Both parties still stood their ground.

Our family and team walked outside and we were standing on the sidewalk when the district attorney walked out. A terse good-bye was quietly exchanged, and he got into his car and drove off. For some reason he felt the need to peel out of the parking lot in front of all of us.

What in the world? Really?

We continued doing private reading lessons and dropping Mason off at school afterward. However, Rick and I weren't thrilled about the cost of the center not being covered by the district. We couldn't understand why money was being spent by the district on an attorney to fight us instead of spending it on a research-based reading program for Mason. The district continued to counter by saying they were providing a research-based program but was unwilling to explain or share it with us.

Exhausting.

At the beginning of middle school we had developed an incredible relationship with the principal. He was extraordinary man and went out of his way to befriend Mason, protect him, and give him an overall great experience. Rick, Mason, and I appreciated him so much. However, due to our disgruntlement at the district level, our relationship was severed. To this day, we feel bad about that.

***

The private reading center—I went to it. Did I like it? Not really. My mom felt like she was helping me with my reading, so I went. It may have helped a little, but I really went to get out of public school. Again, I just played the game.

Seeing the sheriff's car parked in front of the school when we came from the reading program took me right back to Michigan with the officers coming into therapy to visit! My heart began to race. I was afraid to get out of the car. I just wanted to disappear!

I am an upbeat, optimistic person most of the time. I usually can look back and see the beauty after the rain. Not so much in my middle school years. My brain is too fogged by the damage of the storm. I have an extremely tough time appreciating the lessons learned while in school. They took so much away from me. They damaged my heart and soul, and it brings tears to my eyes if I think more than five minutes about my experience there.

I survived middle school, but barely. I struggled with the feeling of being unheard, unseen, and unworthy, and it had an impact on my mental health. It was years of listening to others tell me what they thought I should do, what they thought I should learn, how I should learn it, and what was best for me. If I told them or my mom that I didn't agree with what they were wanting me to do or how they were doing it, it caused rhetoric.

The staff would tell my parents how I never acted like anything was wrong, how I wouldn't say anything to them, so they were shocked when they received an email from my mom. They weren't wrong. I was already a "physical" problem to them, so I put a smile on my face every day. I joked, laughed, and tried to blend in so I wouldn't be more of a burden. But I wasn't happy. My soul was dying.

Eventually I got tired of putting a smile on my face, of being jovial in the hallways just to appease others. I didn't like their teaching style or the decisions being made based on the consensus of the school staff, so I was criticized.

Depression and anxiety, meet cerebral palsy!

***

Mason completed the eighth grade but never received a report card for the year. We asked about it once, but never pursued it. They let him into high school, so we just went with it. Mason's desire to go to school was dwindling. He was holding on to his educational journey by a thread. He was miserable. We hoped high school would be a better experience for him.

***

I still wonder to this day if there is an eighth grade report card on file for me. I think students should be able to grade teachers and give them report cards. Report cards are merely judgments based on so-called standards that provoke a label of below average, average, or above average. Instead of competing, how about we collaborate to meet the standard and devise that plan?

That Makes a Guy Feel Fabulous

In between working, home life, and everyday challenges, I would try to get Mason away from the video games. Through long years of intense physical therapy sessions, home programs, and exercise, it was apparent Mason needed to keep active. Movement helped with his muscles, bones, stamina, function, pain, and further need for surgeries. A teenage boy also needs friends! He needs to be hanging out, laughing, and cutting it up with other guys.

Every quarter, Mason's service facilitator would come to visit, update paperwork, talk about services available, and touch base with us. She mentioned the waiver program would allow us to have a caregiver to help with Mason's needs. She explained the caregiver could take Mason places, do things with him, and help as needed, and his fees would be paid by the county. I was so excited about this for Mason. I thought it would be a great opportunity for Mason to get out, do things, and be with someone other than good ole mom. My best idea was to have the caregiver take Mason to the community gym where they could work out together. Mason can work out, but with most machines and exercises, he needs someone to hold his feet or make sure he is in alignment so that the exercise doesn't cause more damage to his body.

Mason was not thrilled with this idea. He didn't feel comfortable being with someone he didn't know. After much convincing, he agreed to give it a try. The county assigned a young man who was eighteen and a senior in high school to Mason's case. He was African-American, thin, tall, and had an incredible smile. His name was Jimmy. To make sure everyone was comfortable with each other, we decided to do a family outing with Jimmy to the local nature center. It was an early spring day, the sun was shining, and we all piled into my minivan. It was me, my mom, Leah, Mason, Quinn, and Jimmy. Jimmy was not a shy person. He was friendly, talkative, and seemed like a character. I really liked him.

After we parked at the nature center and unloaded everyone from the car, I mentioned that we all should put sunscreen on. It wasn't overly hot, but it was that new season of sun, and everyone's pale skin hadn't been exposed yet. I reached into my tote bag and pulled out the bottle of sunscreen.

Without hesitation, Jimmy shrieked, "Thank you, I will use that!" and grabbed the bottle from my hand. Jimmy applied a lather so thick he now matched all of us! It caught us all by surprise. I was looking at my mom, my mom was looking at me, and Mason was speechless—which doesn't happen often. It was the funniest thing! Now, don't get me wrong, I understand people with dark skin can still burn in the sun, but the enthusiasm and frenzied application were hysterical.

"Here Jimmy, let me take the lotion and start on Mason and Quinn while you get that all rubbed in," I said. My mom offered to help Jimmy get his lotion rubbed in, and he graciously accepted.

The day at the park was fun! Jimmy and Mason walked the nature trails way in front of us. I could hear Mason laughing, and he appeared to be having a great time. It made my heart happy. It's hard to explain to those who don't know or live with a child who has special needs, but simple, everyday joys are intensified when you see them accomplished.

After the day was over and Jimmy had left, I asked Mason about the day and his feelings on Jimmy.

"He was okay," he said.

"What do you mean? It seemed like you guys were having a great time."

"Yeah, he's funny. But I don't know. I'm not sure I want to hang out with him."

"Mason, you are going to give this a try! He is a nice guy. He did great with you today. He will be perfect to work out with. He likes football. He's going to be a lot of fun; you wait and see."

No response, so I let the topic die for the moment.

Jimmy came over one more time to hang out with Mason at our house before taking him anywhere. They played video games and swam in the pool. Again, Jimmy never lacked in personality or enthusiasm. He was a ball of energy. I really liked him.

The next planned visit was for Jimmy to take Mason to the local fitness center. I said if they wanted to get lunch or go to the park or whatever, that was fine too. Jimmy was scheduled to be with Mason from noon to three that day. I knew Mason was hesitant but encouraged him to give it a try. "You don't know until you try."

"Yeah yeah, right, Mom."

I'm not going to lie; it was scary to watch my son walk out to a car and get in with an almost stranger and drive off. My internal dialogue went like this: "You must let him grow up. He cannot rely on and be with you all the time. He will be fine." I then busied myself with housework, playing with Quinn to keep my mind off Mason.

At two-thirty they returned. Jimmy was still happy-go-lucky and chatting about how it had been a day. I thanked Jimmy and told him we would be in touch for his next visit.

"Great!" Jimmy said, and off he went.

Jimmy wasn't even out of the driveway when Mason announced, "There will NOT be a next visit. I am not going out with him anywhere again. And you can't make me."

"What in the world, Mason? What happened?"

I'll let Mason explain.

***

"Hey man, would it be okay if we go get my football helmet before we go to the gym?" Jimmy asked me.

"I guess that would be okay. Where is it?"

"It's at a store downtown called Cook's. I really need to get this helmet for football practice tomorrow."

"Okay."

To get downtown, we went 275 East to 47 and got off at the Sixth Street exit downtown. I was nervous about Jimmy's driving. It felt unsafe. He also was talking hands-free on his phone while he was driving. The conversation was awkward. He was talking to his friend about a double date they had gone on and their thoughts about the girls. I felt like I shouldn't be there or listening to this conversation.

We got downtown and Jimmy was having a hard time finding parking. He asked me if I thought I could walk a little bit. Not to be difficult, I said, "Sure, I think so." We parked in a garage quite a distance from the elevator. Once off the elevator we walked up a hill on East Sixth Street, turned left, then went two blocks down to the sporting goods store, Cook's. The football gear was all the way in the back of the store. I continued trucking on with sweat forming on my forehead, a huff to my breathing, and thoughts going through my head, like "What the hell is happening?" I would have never walked this distance without at least my two canes (yeah, I only had one), and most likely I would have taken my chair.

Jimmy found a salesman and asked him about a certain football helmet. The salesman went into the back and brought out the helmet. Jimmy was very excited, but then realized he didn't have enough money for the helmet.

*He pulled out his cellphone and called his mom. Jimmy pleaded his case
to his mom, saying had to have the helmet by tomorrow but he didn't have
enough money, and could she please help him out. She agreed to give him
the money. A plan was made for him to meet her in Newport, right across
the bridge, so that he could get the money. So . . . I persevered and trudged
my way back to his car.*

*We drove across the bridge and met his mom in the Target parking lot. She
was so nice, happy to meet me, and talkative like Jimmy. We spent a little
while chatting, then she went into mom mode, telling Jimmy that he would
need to pay her back, that money doesn't grow on trees. Again, awkward!*

*The ride back to downtown consisted of Jimmy talking, and talking, and
talking about this football helmet and how bad he needed it, how relieved
he was that he could get it because he didn't think he was going to be able
to because he didn't have enough money. He talked about how practice
started tomorrow and he would be sporting the coolest helmet on the field.
The conversation was one-sided, and I just sat in the car thinking, "I am
not walking to that store again. I just can't!"*

*As he started circling the block to look for parking near Cook's, I spouted,
"I can't walk that far again this time."*

*He said, "I know, buddy, I know. I was thinking I would pull into this No
Parking spot for the few minutes I need to run in there. Okay?"*

*I didn't really know what to say, but I knew I wasn't walking that far
again! So, I nodded.*

*With that, he pulled right in front of the store, left the car running with
me in it, flashers on, in a spot that was clearly marked "NO PARKING."
Do-dah, do-dah. I sat.in.the.car.*

*I watched people walk by on the sidewalk. I watched buses picking up
and dropping off patrons. I was on full alert, just waiting for someone to
knock on my window, not knowing what I would do if they turned out to be
the police or the homeless man in front of me on the corner.*

*After what felt like eternity, Jimmy appeared with a huge Cook's shop-
ping bag and a grin on his face that extended from one ear to the other.*

"Man, I got it! It is dope! I am so excited! I can't wait to wear this to practice tomorrow. Now, let's hit the gym."

Was he kidding me? I just DID the gym walking eight miles downtown. "Jimmy, I'm good. After the distance I walked, I can't work out."

"Are you sure, man?"

"Oh, I'm sure, man."

I don't what happened. I think the excitement of getting the helmet he wanted went to Jimmy's feet. He was now driving extremely fast on the highway. I was afraid to look at the odometer, but it felt like we were going ninety miles per hour. I honestly was scared. He had turned the music on the radio up and was singing loudly, happy as a bug in a rug.

I was anxious and wanted to get home.

***

I couldn't believe what Mason was telling me. These things could not be true. Mason has a history of embellishing things—this story had to be embellished. Had to! I explained to Mason that I needed an accurate and truthful account of what had occurred. I explained to him that I was going to have to call the county to discontinue services with Jimmy and I would need to tell them why. "Mom, what I told you is the truth. I am not exaggerating. I will not, I repeat, will not be going out with Jimmy again."

Great! I had been so relieved thinking I had found some respite for me and given Mason a great opportunity, and it turned into a report. It was the same way with school. I did as much as I could, when I could, but when I reached out for some assistance it turned into a fiasco. Sigh.

The county appreciated my call. They said they would take Jimmy off services for Mason. Surprisingly, they even called back several days later and confirmed that Mason's account of events—minus talking on the cell phone and speeding—was exactly what Jimmy told them.

A MUDDY LIFE

***

A few months went by, and I had the inkling to revisit my idea of a caregiver for Mason again. It seemed like such a great idea; maybe Jimmy just wasn't a fit. I felt it was worth another try, but we'd have to be more selective in our choosing.

At Leap Beyond Therapy, we had volunteers. These volunteers were mostly college students who were accumulating hours for their career path. Most were heading into a medical field or physical or occupational therapy. One day I was talking to Finn, a college student who was studying to become a physical therapist and spent a lot of time volunteering at the center. I asked him about his summer and if he had a job lined up. He explained he was going to work here and there because of summer school. I told him about my idea with Mason, that I was looking for someone to hang out with him, go work out, swim, maybe even spend a day at Kings Island.

"Is something you'd be interested in doing?" I asked Finn.

"I'd love to! How many hours and days are you wanting?"

We discussed the details. I would be paying for Finn out of my own pocket because he was not contracted or employed by the county. Now came the hard part—convincing Mason!

Mason was reluctant. He didn't want to do it, but he knew it meant a lot to me. I talked about how much fun he was going to have, how great Finn was, and that it was going to be a great summer.

***

We did the same thing we did with Jimmy—had Finn come over to the house to hang out and see how things felt for everyone. Finn and Mason hit it right off. They played video games, Finn made them sandwiches for lunch, and Finn even invited one of Mason's school friends over to hang out with them. It felt so good.

After Finn left, I waited for the bombshell from Mason—that he didn't like him or that he wasn't going to hang out with Finn. Much to my surprise, Mason was excited about hanging out with Finn this summer. SCORE!

I had an afternoon work meeting scheduled, so I asked Finn to come over and stay with Mason. It was a hot summer day, and Finn asked if he and Mason could swim. I went over the rules: "Mason is not allowed in the pool by himself for one minute, even if you have to go to the bathroom. Phone needs to be poolside."

Finn asked, "Would it be okay if we invited Nathan over so we could toss football in the pool with another person?"

"Absolutely," I said. "But still, no one in pool if you are not in visual range."

Finn and Mason began changing into their suits. I was rushing around getting dressed for work, gathering my things together, and making sure the guys were settled. I felt a bit overwhelmed attempting to leave, but they were in the pool, and I thought I had everything, so I made my way out to the van.

I threw my things into the passenger seat, got into the driver's seat, started the van, shifted into reverse, and BAM!

Oh my God! What was that?

***

"DUDE! MY MOM JUST HIT YOUR CAR!"

"No, she didn't!"

As soon as I said, "Oh yeah, she did," my mom was at the gate. I don't know whose face was whiter, hers or Finn's. They both looked like they had seen a ghost.

"MOM! Did you hit Finn's car?"

180

My mom was scrambling for words. "I did. I'm so sorry. I'm not used to cars being behind mine, and I didn't look. I'm so sorry."
"Is there damage?" Finn asked.
"I didn't see any, but I will call your parents and talk to them."

***

I left for my meeting shaken, nerves rattled, and feeling over-whelmed. It was the exact same feelings I had endured when Mason was a baby and I drove hit the car in front of me at the ATM.

I called Finn's dad on the way to my meeting. He was so kind and gracious. He said he would come over to look at it after he got off work and we would go from there. I told him I didn't see any damage but I wanted him to look underneath and that I would call the insurance company so we could get things taken care of. He said the car was older and it was meant to get his kids through and college, so dents and scratches were to be expected.

Finn's dad came over that evening and was not concerned with the minor scratches on the front of the car. No lights were dam-aged, and there wasn't any hood or undercoat damage.

Phew! One of the top embarrassing moments in my life!

***

Finn and Mason had an incredible summer. Finn was diligent in taking Mason to the gym and assisted him with his workouts. They went to Kings Island, swam, and Finn even took Mason to his ther-apy appointments for me sometimes.

Mason told me about some awkward times, like when Finn helped him dress and undress after working out or swimming. One time, apparently, they were in the waiting area at the local hospital for Mason's therapy, and Mason thought it would be funny to rip a fart loud enough for the windows to vibrate. Mason told me he thought Finn was going to die; he wasn't sure if it was from laughing or total embarrassment.

Their first adventure to Kings Island was memorable. Instead of taking Mason's wheelchair, they took Mason's scooter. As they made their way to the entrance, they were stopped by park personnel. The person claimed Mason could not take the scooter into the park as it was not medical equipment. Mason and Finn didn't know what to do, so they called me.

"What? Not medical equipment? Then what is it?"

I told Finn that statement didn't make any sense and asked to speak to the park employee. They were not willing to talk to me, so they took the phone into the office to allow me to speak to someone. After explaining Mason's condition and situation, they agreed to allow the scooter in the park. I'm not sure if they were being accommodating or if they didn't want the responsibility of watching his scooter in their office while they used one of the park's wheelchairs.

Despite a few bumps, it was a summer where my heart was full. I loved seeing Mason with Finn going places, doing things, and being goofy young men.

***

My dear ole mom! She does so much for me. I recognize and realize how much work I am for her. It makes me feel terrible, but I don't know what to do about it. Sometimes when she comes up with an idea "for me," I know it is really for her, so I try not to make things more difficult. She fought tooth and nail for me every school year, so I felt like I could at least make her summer less tense.

Let me tell you about my mom's idea, though. While it may have been good in theory, in actuality it was horrible. She was paying someone to be my friend. A paid friend? **That makes a guy feel fabulous!** *She can twist it, boast about it any way she wants, but bottom line? PAID FRIEND.*

Finn and I did have a lot of fun! I joked with him all the time, saying, "Thanks for being my paid friend!" The best part about Finn was he didn't play when it came to giving me a good workout at the healthplex. He increased repetitions and made sure I had a good foundation and was correctly aligned. Every week he added a new exercise. I learned quite a bit from him about how to exercise and work out.

We had several experiences that were crazy embarrassing but left us belly laughing. My mom running into his car? Top notch! I still can't believe there wasn't any damage. The crash, boom, bang sounded like the front end was gone.

When a guy has to fart, a guy must fart! I'm sorry it was in the waiting room. After I did it, Finn yelled at me, "MASON! We are in public!"

"Here's the thing, Finn. When I have to fart, I can't tell you if it going to be silent, loud, short, or long. This one just happened to be loud and long."

Our laughing, snorting, and trying to catch our breath probably was more attention-grabbing than the actual fart.

I did love my time with Finn. We had really good times. For years after, and even once in a while now, we talk on social media. He obtained his doctorate and became a physical therapist. As one with personal experience training with him, I know his clients are going to get the treatment and exercise they need.

Our favorite line to each other is still, "DUDE, SHE JUST HIT YOUR CAR!"

Respect the Differences

We were in a department store shopping with my mom. My mom wanted to go upstairs, and there in front of us was the escalator. Mason was older now. He was grown. His fears of things had lessened, he had more control over his body, and I mean, c'mon, the escalator only requires one step forward to get on and off. I convinced Mason to give the escalator another try. I told him I was there, that I wouldn't let anything happen, and that he could do it!

Adamant and brave, he said, "Okay, let's do it!"

I took his canes in one hand and his hand in the other. As we stood on the comb plate, I gave a stern "step now" instruction.

Mason stepped. The problem was he stepped too far. His foot was at the edge of the next step and as the escalator proceeded, Mason's balance went way off. I was jiggling, pulling, and dancing to get him stable. As I struggled, he grabbed a hold of me stronger. There was no keeping us upright. We tumbled, his cane went a-flying, my flip-flop soared, and my mom gasped in horror as she watched our acrobatic performance.

Not sure where he came from, but store security appeared. He hit the emergency button and helped us to our feet. Thankfully we didn't get hurt. But good grief, were we embarrassed.

"I told you so, Mom! I don't do escalators," Mason yelled at me.

185

I didn't have words. He was absolutely right. He didn't do them—correctly anyway!

The elevators are always in the corners of stores and the escalators are in the center. I tried! I really tried to get him over his fear. At the time I felt convenience was more important than safety. "Get over it, kid! Let's do it!" That didn't prove to be the case for either of us.

***

I just explained how I felt teachers and staff in middle school never listened to me! Here was my mom, also not listening to me.

I do not do escalators!

I like to try to overcome fears because I know fears limit us. So I gave in and tried the escalator thing AGAIN. As you heard, it did not turn out well for either of us.

People, even our own parents, put their beliefs and desires into our heads! There is a fine line between good intentions and trying to transform others into what you think they should be.

Respect the differences, folks.

Got to Take Care of that Smile...

Rick and I met by being set up on a blind date by our friends. When they came to pick me up, Jay and Veronica were in the front seat of the car, and Rick was in the back. Rick enthusiastically welcomed me into the car. He was a thin guy with dark hair cut mullet-style—shorter on the sides and longer in back. The back of his hair was tightly curled, which I later found out was because he had his mom perm it. He looked like a young Rick Springfield. He wore jeans and a t-shirt. It was immediately apparent that he was a kind, genuine, sincere person.

As we talked, he told me about his golden retriever, Brock. I remember responding, "I have a golden retriever too! Her name is Rita."

Sitting by Rick and talking in the back of the car was easy. It was comfortable. However, his smile, although bright, was filled with crooked, unaligned teeth. I remember thinking, *You are too good-looking to have uneven teeth. If this relationship works out, we will be discussing braces.*

After four years of dating and engagement, my handsome groom walked down the aisle with a mouth full of metal to appease his bride.

***

As Leah approached her pre-teen years, we began consulting with orthodontists to make sure our beautiful daughter had the prettiest smile possible. In our community, it seemed like everyone used the same orthodontist. Following suit, we made our initial consultation appointment and began her five-plus years of orthodontic work. We didn't have any problems at this orthodontic office. As with all orthodontic offices, it did seem very production-line-like. Several patients taken back at a time by the assistant and the orthodontist going chair to chair making his recommendations. Leah's teeth turned out immaculate, so we didn't have any negative things to say during her time there.

Fast forward to Mason and his pre-teen years; time to have his teeth looked at. I called the one and only orthodontist, it seemed, in our community. Of course, I did not like to catch anyone off-guard or put them in an awkward situation, so I told them when I called for the appointment about Mason having cerebral palsy, walking with canes, his high anxiety, and just the need to talk through things so he knew what to expect.

"Oh, Mrs. Bailey, that won't be a problem. Thanks for letting us know."

The initial consultation includes photographs of your teeth, x-rays, and even a panoramic screening. All those things require some type of coordination, whether to hold the mouthpiece in place while they put the camera in your mouth, holding the x-ray plate with your teeth in your cheek, and most challenging, standing while the panoramic machine circles your head. The assistant was kind, patient, and really trying to accommodate Mason to get what was needed for the orthodontist. Long story short, the pictures, x-rays and film were not the best.

When the orthodontist came in, he made it abundantly clear that unless Mason could give him good pictures, he would not be able to give us good information. The reason for the pre-call I made, so no one at the office would feel uncomfortable or awkward, had flipped. Now Mason and I felt completely uncomfortable and awkward! The way the doctor spoke to us, as if it was Mason's fault (like he was doing it deliberately), the lack of empathy, and the blatant "you are slowing me and my production line down," left no question in my mind, or Mason's, that we would not be return-ing. The assistant tried to make the awkward encounter better by offering more films and to try again. I simply said the encounter had already been overstimulating and difficult for Mason, and we would just make another appointment.

NOT!

She graciously walked us to the door and off we went.

NEVER TO RETURN AGAIN!

After several months of research, parental referrals, and phone calls, we came upon a female orthodontist about fifteen minutes away. My "Are you okay with this?" pre-call was made to the office. This time, though, I encouraged the clerical staff to discuss every-thing with the actual orthodontist to make sure *she* was comfort-able with Mason coming into the office for treatment.

The office did not call me back. The orthodontist, herself, DID! This doctor was gracious, kind, and wanting to do what she could to not only help Mason with his orthodontic work, but also make sure he was comfortable with it. She was genuinely interested in Mason as whole person, not just in fixing his teeth.

I felt good about going to this appointment. Mason? Not so much. He is a one-and-done kind of guy. He didn't like the way the last office made him feel. He didn't like trying to maneuver that x-ray plate in his cheek, and certainly he did not like trying to stand up straight while the panoramic machine zinged around his head. While going through those stressful things, he heard "not good enough" and knew right away he was not accepted. I get it! Who wants to go through THAT again? I explained to him that all people are different, all experiences are different, and we must give people the benefit of the doubt and a chance. Hesitantly, he agreed to try again.

***

The day before the consultation, the office called to confirm our appointment. They also shared there was a handicap entrance on the side of the building so Mason would not have to truck up the massive number of stairs. I appreciated the call and their kindness.

At the consultation, the orthodontist took time to get to know us, our concerns, our desires, and the challenges to meeting those desires—mental, financial, and physical. She had a calming presence and she did not have an inkling of discomfort with Mason having cerebral palsy. She participated in taking photos of his teeth by holding the mouth guard while the assistant took the photos. She got a chair set up so Mason would not have to stand for the panoramic screening. There was no hurry in her voice, or in her step. She had penciled the time in that we required for Mason to have a successful consultation. She explained to us what she saw and would recommend. She encouraged us to consider doing two three-part treatments to break it up for Mason, which would help us financially, too. She reassured Mason that any time he felt uncomfortable or wanted me to sit by him during treatment it was totally fine. After giving us all her time and the information, she suggested we go home and discuss it as a family and let her know what we would like to do.

Uh, what we would like to do? We would like for you to be Mason's orthodontist and help us reach the goal of a gorgeous smile. Kindness and understanding trumps cost, convenience, length of treatment, and the desire to look at other options.

***

Although Mason wasn't keen on going to his appointments, he handled them like a champ. He knew things would be explained, and that if he was uncomfortable with anything, they would figure it out together. And as Mason does, he made friends with the clerical staff and dental assistants and forged an incredible relationship with the orthodontist. He knew she had his back, so the giggles, jokes, and conversations surpassed the unpleasantness of the oral work. As they got to know Mason better and better, they looked forward to his visits. They waited with bated breath to hear what would come out of Mason's mouth during the visit. He always left them laughing!

The office closed daily for a lunch hour. We had an appointment right after it was over, so we patiently waited at the side door until the staff returned. There was a doorbell you rang to let them know you were at the accessible entrance so they could buzz you into the office. It was a chaotic time as staff was running about returning their lunchboxes to the break room, patients were coming up through the main entrance to the desk, and we were coming in the side entrance; there were just a lot of people in a small area.

As we were bunched together near the handicap entrance, one of the clerical staff jokingly said to Mason, "What are you doing playing the crippled card?" Immediately after she said it, she melted.

Mason laughed and said "You know it! Every day all day."

She quickly rebutted, "I'm so sorry! I was thinking you got hurt during sports. I didn't realize it was you, Mason!"

I remember thinking, "That was odd, but whatever." I never gave it another thought, and Mason seemed unbothered by it. We were part of the family in this office. We knew there was not one person there who would do or say anything to intentionally hurt Mason. As a family, we joke about Mason's disability all the time. As the saying goes, if you don't laugh, you will cry.

As we sat in the chairs across from the orthodontic assistant's desk, you could tell she was distraught. Color had left her face. She was at a loss for words. She stared blankly at us not knowing what to do or say. I wanted to say or do something, but I didn't know what to do either. She was quietly talking to a staff member next to her. I was whispering to Mason to make a joke about it because it was apparent, she felt terrible. Mason wasn't keyed into it whatsoever.

Another staff member called Mason's name to go back for his appointment.

As he went back and I remained in my seat, the young assistant quickly came over and sat next to me. "Mrs. Bailey, I am so so sorry! I should have never said that. I am so so sorry!"

I told her it was fine, and that she really did not offend Mason or me. "We joke about it, too." I told her I appreciated her apology and she asked if she should go say something to Mason. I felt so bad for her that I insisted it was not necessary. Was it inappropriate? Of course, but no one could say or do anything worse than what she was saying and doing to herself!

And, as bad as it sounds or seems, it was taken more as her acceptance of him. There are things you can joke about among friends and family, but if a stranger or someone you didn't know said it to you, it would be more than offensive. If the public heard half the offensive, inappropriate things we say to each other regarding Mason's disability, or my blonde hair, or Rick's forgetfulness, we would be pelted with rotten apples.

At our next visit, Mason jovially signed in and made small talk with the assistant. There was a little awkwardness in the air coming from her, but Mason laughed his way to his seat in the waiting room. The visit after that she wasn't there. We learned she had resigned and went to another practice. My heart told me she left because of that incident and having to see us at visits. I hate that! It wasn't necessary. We were fine. One of those times you have to forgive yourself, accept your own apology and be gracious to yourself about your mistake. We're all human. Mistakes happen. Live and learn. You must move on.

***

At one visit with Mason's neurologist, Mason referred to himself as "Palsy Boy." The neurologist asked Mason to repeat what he said.

Mason said, "I call myself Palsy Boy."

She responded, "Not in this office, you don't!"

Mason's eyes met mine, and I just shrugged my shoulders. Oops!

In my head, I sometimes run through all the inappropriate, crazy things we say, hoping they don't become public. For example, when Mason was opening his lawn care business, the first name he came up with was Crippled Cuts, a play on the name of a local landscaping business—Triple Cuts. We nixed that right away! I'm pretty sure if that was even mentioned to his neurologist, we would have been asked to leave the practice. There is a young entrepreneur who has cerebral palsy and created "Crippling Hot Sauce." I think it's brilliant! However, not all will find or appreciate the humor in it, so we must be aware, gracious, and kind to those who have different beliefs or perspectives. Kindness is the end all and be all.

***

Near the end of Mason's orthodontic treatment, the orthodontist had to cut the main wire to place a new one for the last adjustment before he got his braces off. They were in deep conversation and she was laughing at Mason's wittiness. As the conversation continued, she clipped the wire, and the sound of the clippers ignited Mason's startle reflex, causing him to jump. In reaction to Mason's jump, the orthodontist jumped, and the clippers went flying across the room.

"Mason, are you okay?" she shrieked.

Mason, laughing out loud, said, "Yes, I'm fine. The noise of the clip scared me."

Laughter erupted in the office. That silly startle reflex, it had been forgotten for only a moment. Thankfully, the clippers landed firmly on the floor without impaling any staff or patients!

***

Crooked legs and now crooked teeth! C'mon, gimme a break, people! My internal sense walking into the first orthodontic office was "Nope!" I felt the stares not only from the clerical staff, but all of the patients and parents in the waiting room. Was the assistant nice? I mean, yeah, but it was that "fake nice." You know, the nice that comes because you are totally uncomfortable with the situation and are just trying to get through it. I can tell in a matter of seconds when I walk in a room, or enter a store, or get into a car, the uncomfortableness of the room. Most of the time I can lighten the mood with jokes or kindness, but when it is an uncomfortable situation for me—game over. I am too focused and worried about what they are going to try and do to me to be concerned about them!

I could tell from the very beginning that office was all about numbers. Get as many patients through as you can so the income is higher. The orthodontist was gray-haired, older, had been in this occupation for a long time, and there was no extra room in his schedule for little 'ole disabled me. My inabilities or challenges were not his problem, and he made that very clear. Now, don't get me wrong, he wasn't mean about it, just matter-of-fact, sorry-about-your-luck type of thing. But when you don't have control over having a disability such as cerebral palsy and the coordination of your body, that approach gives you the feeling of not belonging and not being wanted. Okay with me, Doc, I don't want to be here anyway. I can survive with crooked legs, so I can certainly survive with crooked teeth. Bye, Felicia!

I'm glad that my mom understands me and doesn't make me go back to places that are uncomfortable. It isn't good for anyone. Them or me.

When my mom brought up the idea of me going to another orthodontist, I was not thrilled. The previous scenario replayed in my head—Staff acting nice but only really wanting to get the job done. Me and my uncoordinated stance with an overwhelming startle reflex. Just did not sound like a good time. I get that my mom wanted me to have straight teeth, but hey, I want straight legs and that ain't happening.

I agreed to give a new orthodontist a shot. Yee-haw, sounds so fun.

Upon entering the new orthodontist office, immediately different feel than the first one. There was no fakeness, only genuine kindness. I felt welcomed and not a burden. The assistant took my mom and I back to a private room with a reclining chair. She introduced herself and explained what the visit was going to look like and what was going to happen. She praised the orthodontist on her bedside manner and knowledge. She assured us that we would just love her. And we did. She was the real deal. She began with an introduction, asking me about school and what I liked to do. She asked my mom what her concerns were regarding my teeth. She was easy to talk to and surprisingly not in any kind of hurry.

Between my internal knowing when I walked into the room and an overwhelming sense that I could trust this lady, I was all in for my ortho-dontic work.

Every visit I would get some anxiety, still feel uneasy. It wasn't about "going" as such, but more of what was going to happen while I was there. But every visit, the staff would explain to me everything they were going to do. They grew accustomed to my startle reflex, so they were able to anticipate it. I told them even if I knew a noise is coming, I couldn't always control my jumping. They understood.

I became friendly with all the staff there, from clerical to assistants. You could tell I made their day brighter by their enthusiastic "Hi, Mason!" The day that one staff member laughed and jokingly said, "What are you doing, playing the crippled card?" I responded, "You know it! Every day," I didn't think anything of it. Matter of fact, if you look at my dating app profile, you will find the line, "If nothing else, I can provide you with front row parking." It is what it is. You have to laugh at some things or you may cry. People get really caught up in words and wording. I would much rather someone talk to me and be inappropriate than stare at me wondering what to say!

Regardless of words, you got to take care of that smile!

They Didn't Seem to Understand the Assignment

In high school, Mason wanted to try participating on the wrestling team. He was looking for a place to belong. Something he could do among peers outside the classroom. He mentioned this interest to his intervention specialist, and she said she would talk to the wrestling coach. A few weeks later, she took him to wrestling practice after school and introduced him to the coach.

The introduction went something like this: "Coach, this is Mason Bailey. I talked to you about him being a manager for your wrestling team?"

Mason spent the next hour watching the team wrestle. No interaction from anyone. He left. He came home livid that the teacher and coach just assumed he could only be a manager. WTF! (Mason's words this time, not mine). His interest was never mentioned again by the coach or his teacher.

Somehow this experience came up in a discussion with a friend of ours. This friend introduced us to Ellis. Ellis worked with people who have intellectual and developmental disabilities. However, that's not why we were introduced. We were introduced because he was an expert in Jiu Jitsu. Ellis volunteered to meet Mason and assess his ability to wrestle.

That was an unusual meeting.

Furniture moved out of the way. A grown man on our living room floor, ready to wrestle our handicapped son. Haha!

It was a successful wrestle, but at the end of the day, Mason felt the fight for the possible opportunity to wrestle through the school wasn't worth the effort.

***

Ellis made the decision to come and meet me. He knew about Jitsu and wrestling and thought maybe he could help. One decision, based on his passion, rippled into an enormous impact on my life.

Since that wrestling match in my living room, he has become one of my dearest friends and biggest supporters. He hears me. He gets me. His friendship means the world to me. He has helped me to succeed in some things, and in others he has been by my side during the struggle.

Ellis saw me.

Ellis heard me.

Ellis believed in me.

What I said mattered to Ellis!

My opinion was important to him.

Thank you, Ellis! You're da man!

***

One of Mason's high school teachers encouraged him to learn how to navigate the bus system. We weren't opposed to this until we discovered the staff had told Mason he would never be able to drive! That approach hit the brakes for Mason. He refused to learn how to take a bus with the other students. Tell Mason he can't do something and his head spins, figuring out how he can prove you wrong!

We decided to get Mason evaluated for driving. Maybe he could drive, maybe he couldn't. We didn't know. There was a local occupational center that did driving assessments, but it required a prescription. The prescription needed to state the patient's name, date of birth, diagnosis, and "OT/Driving Evaluation." For such a simple thing, I didn't want to make the trip to Missouri, so I made an appointment with one of Mason's pediatricians.

After and hour of talking to the pediatrician about our need to get a prescription allowing an occupational therapist to evaluate him to see if he could drive, she hesitantly agreed to write the prescription. It was an exhausting visit as it was apparent she did not believe it was even a possibility for Mason to drive.

I kept saying to her, "I understand, and he may not be able to, however, that is why we need to do the evaluation."

When we got home, I looked at the prescription, and it read:

Mason Bailey
8-18-1999
Quadriplegic
OT/Driving Evaluation

WTF! QUADRIPLEGIC??

Now granted, this was not Mason's designated pediatrician, but it was someone in the same office who had seen Mason many times over the years. He was in the room during the visit. She had his chart. Did she not know what quadriplegic means?

Script torn up. Proper script obtained from the cerebral palsy clinic in Missouri. OT/Driving Evaluation complete. Mason declared capable of driving with hand control installation.

Take that, doctor!

***

I remember the appointment with the pediatrician and trying to get a prescription to drive. I remember feeling unworthy, incapable, and even invisible.

She would not let it go. She did not think I would ever be able to drive. My mom kept trying to explain to her that we should let the OT doing the evaluation make that call. She was not listening. She had already formed her opinion.

As far as calling me a quadriplegic, again, it was the medical field not being educated properly with those of us who have disabilities. I wish

200

I could say this was a first, but as you have already read, there were many times the wrong diagnosis was given during my upbringing.

Another day, another "you can't do it" moment in my life.

We have such a long road ahead when it comes to medical professionals being able to understand and relate to those of us with disabilities.

I'm happy to say that I drive. I drive a Jeep with hand controls. I'm not sure if that doctor knows or not. I never saw her again after that appointment.

High school was better than middle school, but Mason still felt like he didn't belong. He was placed in small groups of learning. They

had him sorting Skittles for math computations. He would come home sad. He would not want to go to school in the mornings. There were days that required Rick and I to really push the envelope to get him to school. We were suffering as a family. We knew he had to go to school, yet the trauma it was causing him made it hard to send him.

In tenth grade, we sought out treatment for Mason's anxiety and depression. His physician prescribed medication to help him. Within several weeks, Mason's depression worsened to the point of having suicidal thoughts. At the time, we felt it was his depression getting worse.

We did not hesitate to reach out for more help. We took him to the hospital to be evaluated and assessed for his mental health. Mental health evaluations, especially when there is mention of possible self-harm, are very different than physical evaluations. You are stripped down to only a hospital gown, belongings searched, forms filled out and signed. There was even one point when they had a security guard present.

I asked, "Why the security guard?"

The nurse responded, "We do that in case the patient tries to run."

Mason looked at me and we both burst out laughing.

"I don't think he'll be running anywhere. If he does, it will be a miracle!"

It was determined that Mason was having fleeting thoughts of self-harm and had no plan in place. He was referred to an outpatient day program for therapy and counseling.

This was a difficult time in my life. I was losing my happy, go-with-the-flow guy and didn't know what to do about it. For the majority of Mason's life, I had been able to handle things related to Mason. I was creative or reached out and got the support needed, but at that point it seemed reaching out only made things worse. Attempting to get Mason to school and his depression were bringing higher tension back into our home.

***

High school was better than middle school, but still not great. It started out with staff giving me the impression they really wanted what I wanted and what was best to me. That feeling changed as months went on. I began to feel more like a charitable case, as if they were merely doing things to make the school look better not to make it better for me.

The staff were kind and appeared to be my friends. But there was an underlying feeling of being different and being treated differently. The wrestling interest was a great example. "Yes, you can participate; not the way you would like to, but the way we see fit for you."

Every day I would get up and truck into school with a smile on my face, spurting out humor and jokes to get through the day. But by the time I got home from school I was exhausted. I was exhausted physically from walking from classroom to classroom. I was exhausted mentally from trying to do what people wanted me to do and when.

Sadness filled my being, and as much as I tried to hide it, it was consuming me. I was glad my mom saw it and understood it enough to get me medication.

I have always lived in two different worlds. One foot in the physical world. One foot in the spiritual world. It is a conflicting stance and especially challenging because others do not understand or are not open to considering the spiritual side of things. The problems come when people start to debunk things outside the physical realm and become entrenched in the physical reality. In physical reality, my disability defines me. In spiritual reality, I am no different than you.

Unfortunately, the medication my mom got prescribed for me made my depression worse. I began thinking about returning to the spiritual world. I wanted that unconditional love, to be in the no judgment zone again. I began to think the physical world would be better off without me in it. My increased sadness made me not even want to get out of bed. I lacked any motivation and saw no good in the world.

At this point, my mom and dad decided to take me to the hospital, I was in a "whatever" mode. I didn't feel like the hospital was going to listen or understand me any more than my teachers did. The medical staff decided I should attend an outpatient day program, I was all in! As long as I didn't have to go to school, I didn't care what it was.

The outpatient day treatment was short lived. Only four days. The psychiatrist quickly identified that the medication was the reason for my suicidal thoughts and told me to stop taking it. For four days though, I enjoyed the coloring activities, games, and conversations among staff and other patients. It was relaxing. I didn't feel like I had to try and meet anyone's expectations and I could just be.

It didn't take long for the suicidal thoughts to diminish, but the depression remained, some days more than others. My mother and I were reluctant to try further medication since the first one could have had a deadly outcome.

It could be said that my depression was merely a chemical imbalance, but to me it was more than that. I was trying to get the world to become a more loving, accepting place, and find where I actually belonged. I was losing myself. I was so much more than this disabled body, but I was struggling to convince the world of that. School years especially as I was getting older were terrible years for me. Looking back, I still am not sure how I made it through. Now, as my older self, I really wonder if school helped me. Honestly, the fight to get the education, the feelings of not belonging, the mental strain makes me question it.

***

Mason was sixteen years old, and we still were struggling to find something that excited him. Something that made him feel he had purpose, belonged, and was worthy. He was convinced everyone who allowed him to be involved in something was doing it out of pity rather than sincerity. He was tired of being everyone's charity case.

Mason wanted to get a job, and I was all in. I thought it would give him a great sense of purpose and belonging. However, I didn't think it was a great idea to have his mommy trying to help him get employment. So, I set up meetings with the local vocational government assistance program. They were enthusiastic and willing to help us.

SCORE!

However, their help consisted of a job coach taking Mason to different companies, walking in (unannounced), and asking the person at the front desk what kind of work they did there.

Mason came home so mad and embarrassed. "Mom, it was ridiculous!"

One landscaping company they went to was willing to have their boss talk to Mason. Mason wasn't holding out much hope, but the owner of the landscaping company actually called and scheduled an interview with Mason and the vocational job coach. However, it was determined by the job coach that Mason needed to be observed by their staff and the company to determine safety before he could be hired.

We all agreed with this plan.

Weeks went by. Calls were made to the potential employer stating the vocational system was working on having someone come out to see if Mason could do the job, but they were having a hard time finding a staff member who would be available. It got to the point that we felt if we did not react fast, this opportunity for Mason would be over. Rick called the owner of the company directly and asked what he needed.

The owner's response was, "I just need to see that Mason is safe and can do the job. I'm not going to lie, the vocational liaison has me a little freaked out."

Rick laughed and said, "Please do not get freaked out. Mason has been cutting grass and working outside since he was nine years old. I think you will be happy with him and his work ethic."

Rick coordinated a meeting with the owner and had our neighbor, Bob, go with Mason to the meeting. (We felt like Bob knew Mason as well as us, yet he was not "his parent" going on the interview!) That interview included Mason SHOWING the owner that he could use the mower safely, could follow instruction and would be an asset to their company.

Mason was hired at the company and would maintain their six acres of grass! We are forever grateful for this owner being willing to give Mason the opportunity to work for his company! Mason worked at this landscape company for four years. He LOVED IT!

This outcome would have not been the same had we continued allowing the local vocational system to "help" with this opportunity.

That job coach! OMG.

She would walk me into places, unannounced, and introduce herself to the first person at the desk, then say "This is my friend, Mason. Can you tell me what you do here?"

Humiliating!

I was excited when the landscaping company talked directly to me and was willing to give me a shot. But the logistics, delays, and incompetence of the vocational system almost lost the opportunity for me. Again, thank you Mom and Dad for having my back and for assertively taking the reins to get me my first job.

I started by cutting acres of grass. I eventually began using the skid steer for lot clearance and a mini excavator for loading trucks. The employees looked at me as one of their own. I worked two days a week after school for four years. Those four years of work were great! Some of the best years of my working life.

We all have dreams.

We all have desires.

We all have intuitions.

We all have gut instincts.

We all have these things with or without disability.

The voices of other people drown out our inner voice. We can start to believe what other people tell us. Especially if we hear it repeatedly!

*Nay-sayers, I call them! People believe they know what others can and cannot do without giving them an opportunity. **The intervention specialist, the pediatrician, and the job coach did not understand the assignment!***

Give me an opportunity—that was the assignment. Not declare your judgment on me.

Sigh!

Slow the Pusher

During middle school and into high school, there was a family who kept inviting Mason to come try out sled hockey. We did not know about this sport or and even what it entailed. Mason didn't seem all that interested. However, after several invitations and getting invited by others, as well, Mason thought he would check it out.

If you are not familiar with sled hockey it is a sport for people who have limited mobility. Players sit straight long-legged in a sled with their legs strapped; they wear leg pads, helmets, and large gloves. They have shortened hockey sticks that have spikes on one end. The players maneuver the sled by propelling with the spike part of the stick and guides the direction of the sled by leaning their bodies towards the way they want to go. Once near a hockey puck, the player turns the sticks around and uses the blade to slam the puck in the direction of their goal. This sport is not divided out by age like most sports. It is divided out by players' abilities and their skill within the sport. Teams are ranked by novice, beginner, intermediate, and skilled. There are players that even excel into the USA teams and travel internationally to compete. A sled hockey team could have six-year-olds playing among or against fifty-year-olds.

This concept felt strange, but once Mason got into the sled for the first time, he understood! It may sound easy to sit in a sled, but there is coordination and balance needed to stay upright. Then, when you do flip over with your legs bungeed in, you have to o learn how to self-correct yourself in the sled. After you learn to balance, you must add propel yourself with the two sticks by digging them into the ice and allowing the sled to slide. Then, you must learn how to flip your stick over to hit the puck and hit it in the right direction. It is not easy. It is not an easy sport to learn and concur. In combination to all of these things are, there is speed, rules, and player collisions!

Mason was determined to learn this sport after his first night on the ice. He felt freedom in the sled and felt he was playing a real REAL sport! He explained that this team and sport was not like other adaptive sports. He recalls being on an adaptive baseball team that allowed players to run the bases even without hitting the ball. He played adaptive soccer, where basically all the players mobbed around the soccer ball and "tried" to kick it. Neither of those sports felt competitive or real to him. In this sport, he said the ONLY difference compared to a non-adaptive game of hockey was being in a sled; all the other rules applied. Mason attended around six practices before the season of games started.

The first game that Mason played in was in Pittsburgh. If you are not aware, Cincinnati and Pittsburgh are huge rival cities (at least in football). As the game started, my daughter, Leah and I were watching behind the Plexiglas rink side. Rick was helping the players get buckled in and on the ice. Within mere minutes of the competitive game starting, the Pittsburgh fans were pounding on the Plexiglas and yelling, "Slow the pusher! Slow the pusher!" *Bam! Bam!* They continued to pound on the glass. Leah and I looked at each other like "what the heck?"

If a player does not have the physical capability to propel their own sled, then they are assigned a "pusher," a skater that only does that—; pushes the sled. The rule is that the "pusher" of that player cannot skate faster than the opponent sledder. The crowd was yelling at the ref to enforce the rule of slowing the pusher down as they felt he was pushing/skating faster than the opponent.

Leah and I got the giggles.

I said, "Are we at an adaptive sled hockey game or a Steelers versus Bengals football game?"

Leah laughed, and said, "I'm really not sure."

It felt a little over -the -top and obnoxious.

Fifteen minutes into the game, along with the fist pounding and chants, we had now have players slamming into the walls at high rates of speed. We have players in sleds being flipped over from collisions. We had pucks being hit and flying everywhere. And, then Pittsburgh scored! Screams erupted.

I looked over at Leah and said, "This isn't what typical adaptive sports are like. Should I be scared for Mason out there? Because I kind of am!"

At this moment, Rick walked over and joined us. He was as calm as a cucumber and so nonchalant.

"Uh, Honey, should we be worrying about Mason out there? This game seems a little rough!"

"Nah! He' is fine!"

Again, Leah and I just looked at each other with big eyes.

The Icebreakers were defeated by the Pittsburgh Mighty Penguins. Honestly, I was happy about this outcome as I didn't want the Penguin fans to start throwing cans on the ice, or punches, lol!

As Mason came off the ice, he was obviously sweating and had had a workout. The smile on his face told all, though. He was ecstatic and excited about his first sled hockey game. He was all in from there on out!

As his abilities and skills increased on the ice, so did the competitiveness. These sled hockey games were intense!

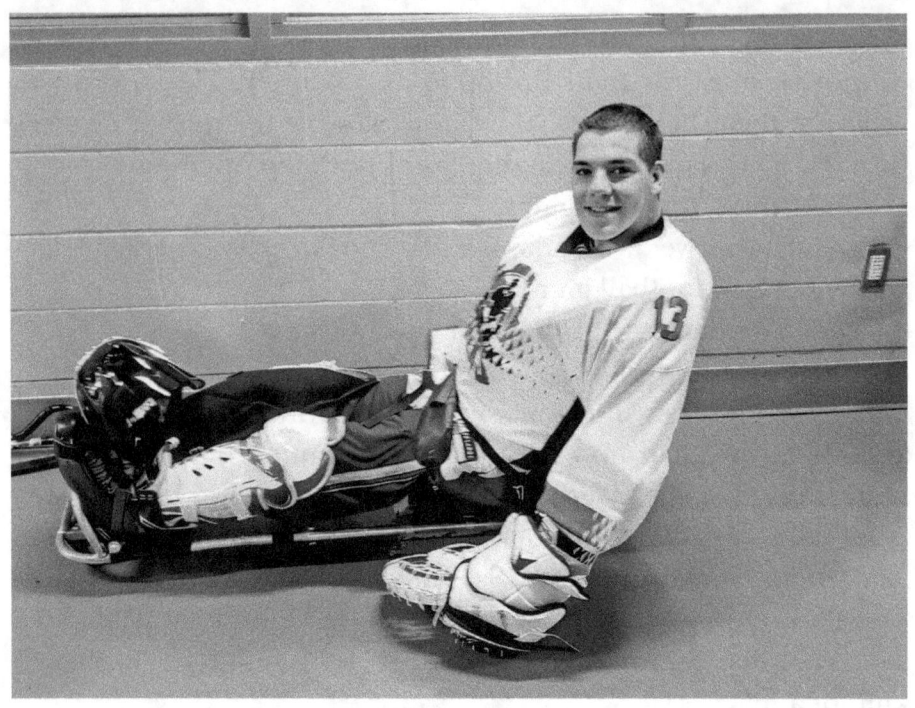

At one particular game, the coach came over to the table of players and announced their goalie was not going to be able to play because he had been admitted to the hospital. He asked if anyone would be willing to play goalie for the tournament.

After several moments of silence, Mason raised his hand and said, "Sure, I'll try it. No guarantees on stopping any pucks, though."

The coach and table laughed.

Mason did as well as he could, not having played goalie before. He loved the adrenaline of being the last-ditch effort before a goal was scored. After the tournament, he asked the coach if he could continue to train as goalie so if it happened again, he would be more prepared. Mason ended up being back-up, then permanent goalie for the Icebreakers for three years. As the years went by,

Mason started to develop pain and physical issues, so he stepped away from the game.

Sled hockey years were some great years for Mason. He REALLY felt a part of something. He reveled in the teamwork. It was particularly a strong time of friendships, pranks, laughter, travel, and competitiveness.

Never heard or seen sled hockey? Look it up! You may be surprised, like I was!

***

Oh my gosh, if this family asks me one more time to come see sled hockey and give it a try, I am going to scream! I didn't really know this guy, he was older than me, but he and his parents were relentless when inviting others to sled hockey. Funny part is…. I now know why! I don't know what my hesitation was or why I was reluctant to give the sport a try but thank goodness I did! Sled hockey is an incredible sport. There is a saying they use "put your disability on the ice" but honestly, it is a sport where you no longer are disabled. Every player is on the same playing ground and grouped by ability and skill. I met people who had spina bifida. I met a gentleman who lost his leg in war. I met others who were challenged by cerebral palsy, like myself. But, on the ice, it didn't matter! We were all about players improving our coordination, fighting for the puck, and trying to out sled the other. In the beginning, it was weird, actually, to be out on the ice with six year olds and forty year olds but at the end of the day all of them, all ages became my friends. Long-term friends. Friends that I am still friends with today.

As far as being a back-up goalie, hell, I will give anything a try once! This is how you learn and grow, by trying new things. I was a little petrified, but when my team rallied behind me with encouragement and praise, I was able to pad up and defend our goal!

It was during my sled hockey years that I felt my body changing. I don't know if it was me growing and maturing or the impact and intensity of the sport. Most likely both. It was at this time I came to realize that I could not always rely on my body. Even when I was younger, when I woke up in the morning it was like opening Pandora's box—what is going to hurt or give me trouble today? During hockey season, pains, traumas (getting pelted in the wrist with a puck), and physical discomforts seemed to be more concentrated.

*I'm not going to lie and tell you that I didn't relish and gloat in the bruises and hematomas. They were marks of honor. I was a man! I was sustaining an injury to win a game for the team! But eventually I came to the conclusion that as much as I enjoyed playing sled hockey, I needed to let it go to protect my body. My body came into this world jacked, so I certainly didn't need to accelerate its course. Late teens into early twenties, I was fully aware that if I wanted to be able to sustain my independence and remain functional, I needed to be cautious and careful with the way I used my body. "Slow the pusher" to my mom and sister had a different meaning than it did to me. I had to slow myself from pushing my body. **In my mind, "Slow the pusher! Slow the pusher!" was me telling me to slack off of this sport.***

I still watch sled hockey on television and root my fellow players on. Shoot! I have team members playing in the US Development Sled Hockey team playing internationally. It is the greatest thing to watch and see them excel. USA! USA!

POOF! Dream Gone!

Remember that sweet little toddler and grade-schooler who was passionate about machinery, grass, dirt, mud, and being outside?

That passion never changed.

He had a dream. A BIG dream! That dream was to be a heavy equipment operator. He talked about it all the time.

In eleventh grade, the vocational school associated with our district had a heavy equipment operating program. Mason was excited and enthusiastically applied for the program.

Several months later, I will never forget that day. I was in the kitchen of our two-story home, and Mason was upstairs in his bedroom. The loudest, most exuberant screams came bellowing down the stairs. I didn't know what the hell was going on. I ran up the stairs as fast as I could.

Mason was in front of his computer just beaming! His face was red, he was laughing and giddy.

"What the heck is going on?"

"I got accepted! I got accepted!"

I still wasn't sure what he was talking about.

He muddled out the words "to the heavy equipment program."

I could not believe it.

I remember his next words: "My dream is going to come true after all."

My heart was full, but still there was a slight wariness in my gut.

Shortly after Mason received his acceptance letter, an IEP meeting determined that it would be best for Mason to do a "shadow" at the vocational school, observing the heavy equipment operating program. Him and I were all about that! What a wonderful way for us to know what kind of accommodation he would need, how the school could adapt things for his success, and how we could get prepared for the next year.

However, that is not how it went. Mason was paired up with an observer who took notes during the class. By "observer," I mean just a staff member the school asked to do it.

Mason told me the teacher was not really interested in helping or changing anything in the class to adapt it for him. Mason said his immediate sense was "this man doesn't want me here." The heavy equipment operations were in the far back of the school lot where there were loads of acreage. Mason asked if he could ride in the gator with the teacher to the area and was told, "No, other students don't do that."

Not knowing any better, we sent Mason to the observation day with his noodle DAFOs (dynamic ankle foot orthotics) inside his steel-toe boots. This inhibited his movements because his boots and the braces worked against each other. As a result, Mason had a misstep onto one of the steps of a machine, which caused the DAFO bracing to snap. The second day of observation, the mud was thick and wet. Mason had a few falls and struggled with walking any distance due to the mush.

After he attended the observation days, another IEP meeting was called. We thought the meeting was to look at accommodations needed and plan for him to be in the program. Unfortunately, the meeting really was to give us an adamant no to Mason attending the program. They deemed him "unsafe" and were unwilling to allow him to try or make any accommodations.

I pleaded for them to have a PT or OT do the observations so they could make suggestions or assess accommodation. I begged for another trial to re-evaluate their safety concerns.

They were not having it! It had been decided—Mason was not allowed to attend the HEO program, period.

Those loud, exuberant screams from Mason's room weeks earlier were now bellowing sobs escaping from him across the table. As a strong person, nurse, fixer, and problem-solver, I normally control my emotions quite well, but I was not able to this time. I began to sob just as hard as Mason and had to excuse myself from the room to try to collect myself.

Mason's one and only thing since he was three years old was denied.

Mason was done with school. D-O-N-E! He felt he was only going to school to do what they wanted and he was not going to do it anymore!

I remember after they told Mason he was not able to attend and we had gotten our emotions together, the representative from the vocational school commented, "Mason, you know you have a disability, right?"

I remember being confused by that statement.

She continued. "There are programs at our vocational center for people who have disabilities. Project Search and Career X help students find opportunities and do career exploration."

Mason didn't miss a beat. "I don't need to explore a career. I know what I want to do and that is work heavy equipment. I need someone who will give me the opportunity to try. But you certainly have made it clear that you and your school are not willing to do that. I don't want to be grouped. That's all this district does, group me."

I was proud of him for speaking up. Speaking the truth.

I interjected. "We are simply looking for a program that is willing to make accommodations for Mason to do what he wants to do while being among others doing the same thing."

With that, we excused ourselves from the room.

***

I don't know how, but we got him through eleventh grade. We knew it was important for him to graduate with his diploma. We felt that with him having a disability, not getting a diploma would increase his limitations even more. So, we pushed and encouraged every day to get him to school that year.

At the end of the summer and beginning of Mason's senior year, we called a meeting with the high school, vocational school, and our advocates to try to develop a plan for Mason's senior year. Unsurprisingly, no one had reached out to us. After the meeting declaring Mason could not attend the HEO program and the emotional distress caused, there was silence. No emails, no phone calls, no interest in checking in or being proactive for the upcoming year.

In our summer meeting, everyone could see Mason and our distress. The representatives from the vocational school took it upon themselves to apologize for not being able to allow Mason into their HEO program. They went onto say they would be more than willing to look at other programs at their school for Mason.

Mason spouted out, "I am not going to Career X or Project Search!"

"No, I was not referring to those programs. I was referring to other programs at our school."

He had my attention. "What are you thinking?"

"I don't know. Maybe the culinary arts or welding program," the director of the vocational school suggested.

I about choked!

"You actually think that Mason participating in a welding program is safer than operating a heavy equipment machine?"

Crickets.

"I would much rather my son fall off the steps to a machine than be unstable holding a scalding hot torch of fire."

Silence.

"Culinary arts? He isn't interested in that type of work. Plus, that involves knives and carrying plates over to the stove." Snarkily, I said, "Not safe."

I didn't know if these people, who were representatives for the students, were being funny or serious. It was as if they knew they were wrong but their hands were tied.

The meeting was not going well so we had to change directions. Mason had enough credits, and the district recognized his struggle to attend school, so the meeting ended with allowing him to only take the needed classes and leave at lunch. I really do not believe Mason would have finished school if they would not have given him early release.

We ended up filing a civil rights complaint against the vocational school. It took three years for our complaint to be reviewed due to the amount of cases they had to review and the small number of staff members they had working. Upon review, the vocational school was required by law to change policies and protocols and improve the admissions process for people who have disabilities. It didn't help Mason, but we were hopeful that it would help others who might go the direction Mason wanted to go.

***

If there is a feeling I love most, it's the "counted out" feeling. It really gives me the motivation to put everything into that "counted out" task! If anyone knows anything about being counted out, that would be me! I was counted out in school—certain things not accessible, certain people and systems not willing to let me try. I was getting counted out on everything I tried or wanted to do in a brief period of time.

Rejected!

Denied!

Unsafe!

Incapable!

It was starting to wear me down.

When my ultimate dream of operating heavy equipment was crushed, I went back to questioning my purpose in life. They were not even allowing me to try! I was left feeling bitter and angry. I knew there were other students like me who had dreams, and I knew their dreams would not be achieved either. School systems, organizations, and those "trying to help" were failing all of us!

I felt all the feelings. I spent time erasing the negativity and nay-sayers from my mind. I knew and still know I am here to grow.

I know I am worthy. I know I am capable. I know I am deserving. We all are. Yet, I remain bound by societal stereotyping.

Poof! Dream gone!

He Believed in Me, and I Did It!

After Mason's heavy equipment operating dream was shattered, Mason's dear friend, Ellis, continued to research options. Ellis came across an HEO program in a county over from us after Mason graduated. It was an adult career center school. Ellis contacted the school and talked to the instructor directly. He explained Mason's disability, his experience in high school, and the impact it had on him. Ellis got Mason an appointment to go to the school to discuss the requirements and meet the instructor.

Mason was hesitant. He didn't trust anyone anymore, especially at a "school." He didn't trust people who said yes because he felt like it always eventually turned into a no. After much convincing and reassurance, Ellis got Mason to go to the meeting. During the meeting, Mason was asked to ascend and descend the stairs on various heavy equipment machines. He had to take three WorkKeys exams (basic math, language, and comprehension test), which he passed with flying colors. The meeting ended with the instructor, Daniel, stating that he had no hesitation or qualms about Mason coming into the program.

I take that back, Daniel had only one qualm, which he told Mason upfront: "I have back problems and just had surgery, so I won't be picking you up if you fall in the mud."

Mason's response? "Deal!"

Mason and Daniel developed a relationship that not only encouraged Mason daily but provided him with laughs day after day. Daniel always encouraged Mason to be "a loving asshole," and said that's what he was. He allowed Mason to use the gator for long distance excursions, but other than that, Mason did not require any further modifications. When Mason would take a tumble in the mud, Daniel would giggle and say, "Mason, you're not going to get paid if you lay around in the dirt!"

Mason ate lunch in Daniel's truck many days. They would share stories and compare their bouts with pain and how they dealt with it.

Mason excelled in the heavy equipment operating class. He did not have any accommodations in place for testing. He got the grades! Mason inspired Daniel and the other students.

June 2019, Mason received his six certifications as a heavy equipment operator. This never would have happened if Daniel had not been willing to give Mason a chance. He believed in him and he did it!

After completing the program, Mason had to have surgery on his foot for a bunion and malalignment of toes. The plan was after Mason's recovery, Daniel would help Mason find a job. Mason had his surgery in November.

In late November of that year, Mason underwent surgery for a bunionectomy and fusion of his toes. The bunion on his foot and malalignment of his toes caused him to have to "wide spread" his foot. Having his foot in this position put pressure on his knee.

It was an extremely unpleasant surgery for Mason. It required pins being placed into his toes. He was non-weight-bearing for six weeks. It was painful, inconvenient, long, and physically taxing on the family. But, as with all things, we made it through.

After the healing process came the recovery, which consisted of Mason learning how to walk using his "new foot" and developing stamina. The more he stood and the more he walked, the more it swelled. It was months and months of getting used to it and finally being able to not think about it.

***

In the scheme of all my surgeries, this one seemed less involved. But I am here to tell you, when someone is messing with your ability to walk or be independent, there is nothing "less involved" about it. Six weeks of non-weight-bearing meant total care being given to me by my parents, from showering to wiping my ass. I played video games until I wanted to puke.

As with most of my surgeries, I can handle it for the first two to three weeks, but come that fourth week I am miserable. And I make those around me miserable.

It was exciting when it was time to get the pins out and I could weight-bear finally . . . only to be crushed all over again. I had to work extremely hard (and it was slow) to get back to where I was. It hurt to put weight on my foot. My foot swelled when used. I had a new gait, which meant I had to learn how it all worked together.

Joy!

***

December 24, 2019, I sent a text to Daniel that read "Merry Christmas to you and yours!" It wasn't even a few minutes, and my phone rang from Daniel's number. It was his wife, Marcia. Marcia explained that she just received my text and was sorry to inform me that Daniel had suffered a hemorrhagic stroke. She went onto elaborate that due to the significant hemorrhage it would be a long road to recovery.

Six months later, at the age of fifty-five, Daniel passed away.

***

There have been three heart-stopping experiences in my life.

The first time my heart stopped was when I was in my room and opened the email stating I was accepted at the vocational school for the heavy equipment operating program.

Pure bliss heart-stopping moment!

The second time my heart stopped was at the table in my high school when the district told me I would not be allowed to attend the program due to safety concerns.

Anger cardiac arrest.

The third time was when I lost Daniel.

Sudden, shocking, flat-line.

Loss is hard. It hits your heart, soul, and every ounce of your being. As a spiritual person, I know Daniel is in a better place. A place of unconditional love. A place we all came from and a place we will return to. I know part of Daniel's life purpose was to give me an opportunity and help me fulfill my dream, and I am forever grateful for that. All this knowing still doesn't make the heartache and grief, even for me, easier.

Daniel believed in me. He knew I could and would accomplish my dream to operate heavy equipment. He was my right-hand man! We shared so many stories, laughs, learning experiences, and fun.

Thank you, Daniel, for believing in me. Because of you, I did it—I became certified in heavy equipment operating.

Daniel, I also want you to know that I am doing as you taught me and continuing to be a "loving asshole." Ha! Although I didn't have to tell you that because you remain by my side to this day, just in spiritual form.

Cerebral Palsy Wins Again

After Mason recovered from his foot surgery, he was ready to start job hunting! He was so excited to try and find a job where he would be doing what he was passionate about—operating heavy equipment!

With severe hesitation, we reached out to the local vocational system again to help Mason find a job. We expressed our concern and explained how the last time we used them it almost cost Mason a job. They assured us they understood and would do better.

After months of perfecting the resume and practicing interviewing, Mason was sent out for interviews. They were all the same. He walked in, mouths dropped open, amusement about what he was wanting ensued. Mason did his absolute best to explain his abilities, his passion, and his disability. Each interview ended with disappointment, humiliation, and defeat.

Before Mason was comfortable with long distance highway driving, I drove him to an interview in Kentucky with a concrete company. As I waited in the car, I prayed for a positive experience for Mason. It ended up being the exact opposite. Mason came out devastated. Tears running down his cheeks, words incomprehensible, snot flowing. He told me it was his last interview. He refused to put himself in a position again to be humiliated and embarrassed by an employer blinded by his disability.

The interviewer had blatantly told Mason, "We would never hire you here." He was done!

I don't know if you noticed, but Mason is an easygoing, keep trying kind of guy. He gained this quality from me. We both have patience of gold and we can take a lot, but once we hit our emotional limit—game over.

He had reached that point. Once he is done, he is done (with that path at least).

* * *

I really, really thought my schooling would land me the job of my dreams! I thought those certifications would speak for themselves, and an employer would see my value. All my life has been spent proving myself to others. Now I had papers with legitimate concrete proof. Not just my word, or someone else's word, but a National Center of Construction Equipment Research certification showing I was able to operate heavy equipment following Occupational Safety and Health Administration (OSHA) guidelines.

I went to at least ten interviews, and not one person in those interviews saw any value in having me work for their company. All the interviews were the same—me explaining my disability and how I overcame it, and them stating some version of "I do not think you are a good fit for our company."

That interview at the concrete company was awful! The dude told me that I couldn't lift things or maintain the truck, and that I pretty much had wasted his time for coming in. I left bawling my eyes out, and nothing my mom said meant anything to me!

After we got home from the longest, most heartbreaking drive following that excruciating interview, Mason received a call from a landfill five minutes from our home wanting Mason to come in for an interview. His tears dried up so fast! He was pumped, and they were willing to see him that day.

That was the best interview Mason ever had, because it went like this: Get in the machine and let us see what you got. He climbed up in the front loader grinning from ear to ear. He showed the interviewer he was capable, able, willing, and good!

He hired Mason on the spot, and Mason worked there for three months. He enjoyed it, but it was not the best situation.

I will let him explain.

***

There is no better feeling than the feeling of being given an opportunity! When that employer said to me, "Show me what you got," during the interview, I knew I would get the job! It was like my battery-operated-toy days. I was free and seen without disability. I was capable.

In a matter of hours, my deepest, darkest self changed to my most elated, joyous self! It's funny how fast life can change. It only takes one minute, one gesture, one word, and your life can become different. That is why we must live moment to moment. There is something in all of us that realizes even when the dark clouds come, there is light within us.

I was hired at that landfill company to drive the front loader. I would unload trucks and move contents into the landfill. For three months I worked from six in the morning until four, Monday through Friday. Truck after truck came in to empty their contents; I would log if it was wood, metal, or plastic; I regulated the truck traffic because it could get backed up.

I'm not sure if you have ever driven a front loader, but it is a bouncy ride. Ten-hour days and continual bouncing were taking a toll on my body. While I loved every second of it, it was also brutal on my knee. But hey, that was okay! I continued to show up for work morning after morning. I continued putting my ten-hour shifts in and enjoying my customer contact.

The landfill company was run by the son of the original owner. My boss was only a year or two older than I was at the time. He was extremely nice, but green. He tried, but the company was not organized, to say the least. If you know me, I make the best of any situation that I can. There were two guys that I developed a decent friendship with. The company had many contract workers who divided out the contents for recycling purposes. Some of these guys only spoke Spanish, so I got to learn some hand signs and Spanish to talk to them. I loved that!

I was expected to eat my lunch in the machine. They even encouraged me to relieve myself from the side of the front loader instead of taking the time to get off the machine and walk into the restroom. It seemed over the top, but I was not willing to give up. I was in my element, and I looked forward to work every day.

My body began to ache increasingly each day. I was really feeling it in my legs, especially my right knee. When using the gas pedal, it is innate for your foot to go up and down. This motion is called dorsiflexion. This is a motion that is difficult for me to do and requires strong attention for me to do it. The repetitive movement of dorsiflexion, bouncing, and the position of my leg was causing torque to my knee ten hours a day, five days a week. I ignored the pain and continued to give it my all.

One day I went to the boss and asked if I could be trained in the excavator, which is hand-control operated, thinking it would get me away from the repetitive motion to give my knee a break during the shift. I also asked if we operators could cover each other's breaks instead of being interrupted by customers while on them. He denied my requests.

If there is anything I do not want, it is to feel "different" or need accommodations because of my disability. I'm always in "prove myself" mode because my experience has been that society says, "Those who have disabilities are not worthy." Not worthy of adjustments, changes, or adaptations.

Not one person at this landfill had heavy equipment certification. All were taught on the job and, like I said, grew up around the company.

My suggestions and willingness to try to help protect my body so I could continue to work were overlooked.

One day at four o'clock, I pulled the front loader over to the elevated stairs used to get into the top loader. This platform is where I left my cane. As I grabbed my cane, I noticed the handle part was slick. Some asshole had put oil all over it. I'm sure it was meant to be funny, but it was not cool. It was

not a loving asshole move. I told the owner, but he was at a loss as to who it could be or how to handle the situation.

I never did find out who did it.

***

Three solid months into the job one of my knees was compromised. It hurt so bad. It was tight, swollen, and would not bend freely. I tried to self-recover with hot baths, early bedtime, and doing nothing on the weekends to prepare for the next work week. It did not work. The pain was too severe for me to take. It got to the point where I could not walk because of it. I had to call off from my shift.

One day of calling off led to another day, and another. I had been off for a week.

My pain was minimally better, but my mental health was getting the best of me. My mind kept telling me, "They're right, I am not worthy." "I am not capable." "I'm not deserving." All the things I know are not true, but can feel true in times like these. Every day, all day, I try so hard to prove myself to people, only to disappoint myself.

My boss from the landfill called at the beginning of the second week to inquire about my pain. When I told him I didn't know how long it would take to recover and that I would be back as soon as I was able, he said he could not hold my position and that he would have to fill it. That was it. No further contact with him or the company.

It made me feel extremely important to them. NOT!

It was at a doctor's appointment during that process of healing that the doctor stated this motion could very well wreak havoc on a typical person, but because of my cerebral palsy, the long hours of not repositioning and not walking or taking breaks torqued my knee. And since I kept pushing through the pain, I made the situation worse. As always, my family and supporters rallied around me. It took several months for me to get over the injury to my knee. I was in physical therapy, using heat, elevating, and taking NSAIDS for months until that knee decided to heal.

First I can't get hired because I have cerebral palsy. Then I can't continue to work because of my cerebral palsy.

***

Life does not want a whole bunch of carbon copies. Life does not want you to be anyone other than yourself. The problem is, we exist in a culture where who you are now, your natural self, is not enough. We spend half of our lives trying to fit in and, to a certain degree, be like everyone else. We want to belong. We want to feel loved. We want to feel accepted. But, later down the line, because of life and others' demands, you will start to give up on what's inside of you. If you don't share who you are with those around you, you start to get anxious, neurotic, you start having physical ailments, and you will deteriorate. I did. Life lessons. Take what is inside of you—that only you can share and that only you can give to the world—and that you give it. There is a time in your life that you have to take all the goodies the world and life has given you and synthesize them into medicine. A medicine of learning that only you can share with the whole world.

I am still trying to teach this method to my mom. She wants to give people a chance when we hit roadblocks or bumps. She wants to give them the benefit of doubt. I'm over it. I know who I am. I know what I need and don't need. I am done listening to others tell me what they think is best for me. I'm tired of trying to make things better when it falls on deaf ears.

I have done and continue to do a lot of things because of my mom. I want to make her happy. I want to think maybe that whatever resource she is seeking will make her feel better in this challenging scenario. I don't want to fight with her. I know that I am a lot. I know that I'm a lot of work even if I'm not as much work as others who have cerebral palsy. So, I go along. I abide. I pretend.

Don't get me wrong, there have been people and systems that have helped me. But the lengths and measures I have had to go through have not been helpful. They are judgmental. They are not authentic. They make me want to disappear. I don't know other people who have to sit at a table and be judged or assessed on a regular basis for school accommodations or equipment healthcare needs.

It is exhausting.

Cerebral palsy wins again. *Ugh!*

I'm the Only Approval I Need

Months turned into years after Mason earned his heavy equipment operating certification. He continually talked about how much he wanted to work in the industry. As we drove by construction sites, he would question why he couldn't be doing what that crew was doing.

I continued to encourage him to think about interviewing again. He refused. He said he was done trying to convince people to see his worth.

In the summer of 2022, Mason decided to open his own business: Seasonal Impact Lawn Care. He claimed that by opening his own business he would be able to do his own thing. He would not have to explain himself to anyone or ask for accommodations because he knows what he needs. He could monitor his body and plan accordingly. He was not wrong. He had awesome points.

I hate that although he enjoys this type of work, it is not what he really wants to be doing. I hate that people squashed his dream after he worked so hard to prove others wrong. I hate that employers will not hire him due to their discomfort and lack of education.

He hopes one day to grow his business so he will be able to buy more equipment and do land clearing. But, with dreams and tenacity come hurdles and roadblocks. For every step forward, there are three, four, even fifty steps back.

I always felt if I could get Mason through this one thing, we would be golden. Or if we overcome this, it will be better on the other side. But with every one thing, there is another thing, or two, or hundred. That is how it works with cerebral palsy.

Now that Mason has reached adult age, his income is closely monitored by the government. If he works over a certain amount each month, he loses his benefits. There is nothing Mason and I would like more than for him to get off government assistance; however, and I don't think people realize this, it's not always about the financial assistance, it's the healthcare assistance! The application process for government assistance can take years and is not easy! So, losing their assistance can be detrimental to those with disabilities.

Many believe people with disabilities do not want to work, they just want to get the "free" money. This can't be further from the truth with Mason. There is nothing he wants more than to work. He loves to work! It is difficult to understand the process related to getting government support and still be able to work. Every time I think I start to understand it, there is a caveat that comes up and dismantles my understanding. Government support is not only money, it is also healthcare insurance. It takes years and years to get approval to get government support, whether it is financially or with healthcare benefits. If you lose one, such as the financial piece, then you lose the other, which would be healthcare. If you make over a certain amount of money in a specific timeframe, it excludes you from receiving healthcare, services, and even disabled adult child benefits when the parents retire. It is not an easy process to understand, much less live under.

I remember a meeting with the county where we all assembled around the table. The financial person stood in front of a white board and laid out all the restrictions to government assistance.

She was an expert in the field and knew the information like the back of her hand. However, she quickly became frustrated with my application questions. She would reiterate over and over again, "These are the rules and you must follow them."

I got that part. I was wanting them to help me understand how to practically make these rules work for Mason's situation. Again, they continued to repeat the rules. I reiterated that I wanted to know how to get Mason as independent as possible because his dad and I would not be here forever.

The financial liaison for the county said, "You may need to consider placement for Mason. Mason is only allowed to make this much. The laws are the laws."

Emotions got the best of me, and I belted out, "YES, I KNOW! I am not wanting to not follow the laws or rules. What I want to know is how do we fucking apply these rules to Mason and his self-employment? How can Mason work and not lose his health-care benefits, and be okay when we pass?"

The room went silent. My outburst was neither appreciated nor well-received. Mason's face had gone white from the mention of him being placed somewhere when we passed. Ellis was in the meeting and did his best to smooth things over and get more answers, but it was clear the meeting was over.

I did extend an olive branch by sending an apology email to the group in regards to my outburst. It wasn't long after that we received the email stating they had given us all the information they could, and if we needed anything else to please seek legal counsel.

***

I have found raising Mason that there are people who stand by our side and love unconditionally, while others judge, confront, and leave as soon as they can because we are too much for them. I really am not trying to be difficult. I am wanting support, guidance, and help in meeting Mason's potential. The problem is Mason's potential gets evaluated and determined based on what others believe it should be versus what Mason and I believe it can be. Systems and organizations that are meant to help make it so complicated you can't even understand what they are trying to say or do to help. It is exhausting!

That is how cerebral palsy works—constant trenches through mud!

***

County workers. School employees. Service facilitators. Vocational mentors. Systems. Organizations. Schools. They all have boxes that require check marks. They all have policies, procedures, and opinions, and if you don't fit in their box or they can't put a check mark, they change the need so that they are able put a check mark!

I've never fit into any of the boxes, whether at school or within the county. There is never a "solution" or "place" for me. It makes me feel more broken than I already am. It is a constant parade of people continuously asking me to change myself to fit into their plan. Change myself to meet the dollar amount. Change myself to do what works for what that person says works for them. Not because something is wrong, not because we haven't done something right, not because there is something within us inherently flawed, but because it is simply a change of season.

What if we could lean into all this stuff without boxes, check marks, attitude, and judgment? What would happen if we could approach this type of work from an empowered place of trying to make changes because of the divine manifest? What if you thought of yourself as creation in action and it's time to do what is right for this person in front of me right now?

Nothing is simple on this Earthly world. My dream of operating heavy equipment continues to be postponed.

Hey, it's okay. Honestly, a sense of relief has overcome me. As much as I want to operate, the constant pressure to perform and prove (and prove and prove) my abilities and worth is heavy to carry day after day.

I made the decision to not to let myself down. I opened my own business, cutting grass. It is called Seasonal Impact. It allows me to continue to be outside. It puts me on a zero-turn mower, which gives me freedom from my disability. I have befriended neighbors and I help them with their yards.

While I have disappointment from not doing what I really want to do, I am not fretting about the small stuff.

I am happy. I am content. I am living life. ***I am the only approval I need.***

I Am Not The Problem

It was a typical day, nothing out the ordinary. We were leaving to run errands, and Rick and I had gone out to the car to wait for Mason. Mason finished putting his shoes on, closed the front door, and hustled down the sidewalk with his glowing smile. Out of nowhere, it hit me! Sadness. The feeling of it all being unfair. My heart ached to see my son trudging towards the car with a cane! I looked at Rick, who was unaware of my feelings. I looked at Mason as he put his cane in the car and got himself in. Unawareness.

I realized that although brief in their passing, my inner thoughts could wreak havoc quickly. *I must breathe. I must refocus my thoughts. I must change the feeling of sadness to gratefulness, because I am beyond grateful.*

***

Self-sabotaging thoughts. "Why me?" "This is unfair." "I must be the problem." These three thoughts I abolished very early on in my life. I know why it is me—I am divinely led to be a messenger of love and a teacher. It is not unfair, because as I chose to come into this world. **I am not the problem, as no gift of life is a problem.** *It starts with me. The only thoughts should be of positivity and forward thinking. If they are not, then they will stall your* *growth and being. The Divine doesn't make mistakes. The Divine knows the story and purpose. It is not always easy. Life can be hard. But it starts with your own thoughts. Do you want to propel forward, or do you want to stay tangled in muck that will keep you stagnant, not going anywhere?*

As my mom said, these thoughts can pop out of nowhere. They can attack when you least expect it. Be the protector of your own self care and well-being. As you have read, I have shared my own struggles with my thoughts. You cannot share your light if you allow it to be dimmed with self-sabotaging thoughts.

Max Out Your Life in the Mud

Looking back over the years of raising Mason, there are not too many things I think I would have done differently. Honestly, I am 1000% confident I did the best for him at the time with the amount of knowledge I had. However, as I have written some of our stories and relived our trials and tribulations, I reflect on the "fights." Advocacy and constant pressure to meet the needs of our son was physically, mentally, and financially exhausting. Some improvements came out of them, but often there was loss of relationships and time, and isolation.

We were judged by our local hospital for using out-of-state services and physicians. We were judged when we pushed for what we felt were basic accommodations in school, and legally required. We were judged as we asked for financial assistance with home modifications, adapted equipment, or help understanding government processes.

We have witnessed a multitude of people run away as fast as they can based on our emotional outbursts or frustration. This is easier for them rather than providing us with empathy or compassion. We have had to introduce out-of-the-box thinking and ways to promote advanced treatments. I am so grateful for the families that I was able to help find the resources needed for their children

In the big picture, I'm not sure the advocacy and changes I've participated in have had lasting effects. My heart hurts for families like ours who have to advocate, fight, and persist to get basic needs met for their children, whether that is in a school building, community, or even at home with equipment or adaptations. It is a life long process and can feel isolating and that of despair. I am so grateful though for those life long friendships, and you know who you are! I am indebted to those of you who have not wavered—through good times and bad times.

We worked so hard to have others see Mason through our eyes. We wanted them to see his determination, persistence, and potential. Regardless of whether it was the school, county, employer, or a person on the street, there was such difficulty showing them his worth.

For the last two decades, I have tried to champion awareness, education, improvements, creativity, and willingness to be more accommodating, accepting, and encouraging of people challenged by disability; all while meeting Mason's needs and helping him reach his potential. I was fighting for the greater good for all who were with him or would follow him.

Our journey has been a story of falling through the cracks of organizations, groups, and laws. It has been a constant battle of dealing with others' expectations versus ours or Mason's. Most of the time, when I had hit my limit of energy, knowledge, or expertise and reached out for help with his education, the work force, or county services, the situation at hand got messier and worse. I reflect on these situations often and still can't understand how or why that happened, but it always did. Mason would warn or tell me not to reach out, and yet every time I expected it to be different or a better outcome. It goes along with the saying "Doing the same things yet expecting different results."

Along our journey, I always had others who shared in Mason's struggles at the forefront. Just as I believed Mason needed SDR surgery, intense therapy, and educational accommodations, I knew there were other families and children challenged by the same things.

We shouldn't have to fight for the things we're fighting for just to give our kids the same opportunities as everyone else. We may have won some battles, but it still feels like we lost the war. Regardless of equal opportunity and ADA laws and regulations, society hasn't bought into the value of human diversity. Now, in 2025, politics aim to and are having some success with rolling back civil rights for many. I do not understand it!

I could not be prouder of Mason and his accomplishments. He has overcome more challenges in his short lifetime than a person in their eighties. He continues to smile, laugh, and find humor in the hard stuff. I will not lie and tell you his journey hasn't been hard on him. The battles and having to prove himself all the time has been a mental challenge for him. Challenges that sticks with him to this day- not being heard, not being valued, and immediate anxiety when it comes to during with medical issues and things that remind him of issues that he dealt with at school.

I can only hope that we have a left an imprint for change. As muddy as this life has been, I would not have changed it. I have met the most amazing people, learned more than I ever thought I could, accomplished things I never would have known were possible, and have a more expanded love and appreciation for life—both mine and others.

***

It has not been easy being born with cerebral palsy. People ask me if there was one thing I could change about having cerebral palsy, what would it be. They are surprised when I say my startle reflex. An overactive startle reflex makes me throw coffee when the dog barks, my body goes into overdrive when a horn honks, and I drop anything I'm holding when someone raises their voice and I'm not expecting it.

The change I would like to make would be not to the diagnosis but to life lived around the diagnosis. It has taken me years for me to rediscover myself and my purpose. School had a negative impact on my self worth and well-being. I have post-traumatic-stress-disorder from it. Sounds silly, but it is real for me. Small things can occur and I will feel my overdrive kick in like it did in school. I wasn't listened to. I wasn't included. My opinion didn't matter. I was never enough. I didn't feel worthy.

I will never forget a huge meeting of school personnel, my parents, and my advocacy team discussing what I wanted to do when I grew up went from me saying I wanted to operate heavy equipment to them wanting me to get a job at Lowes watering plants. They said, "You have to start some-where." That meeting resulted in me enrolling in a class to get certified in driving a forklift. Proving myself.

No matter how hard I worked, how much I proved, it didn't seem to matter. Still doesn't. Labels, judgments and limitations still hinder me. Having to fight for simple things, having to prove myself to others, and having limits placed on me all the time killed my soul and dimmed my light.

The past few years, I have had to rediscover my spirit, my light, my worth. I have had to meditate, breathe, and reconnect with my importance and my magnificence. I let the negativity of the world, the nay-sayers, and the systems try to define who I am to be. I refuse to try and prove myself to others anymore; I am the only approval I need.

I have found a new outlet to express myself through sarcasm on Tiktok. It feels good to be myself and not worry about if I offend others or not do whatever it is the way they think I should.

Many people tell me I'm an inspiration. I don't try to be an inspiration; I don't want to be an inspiration. I just want to live my life like everyone else is.

My life can be viewed as muddy because I was born with a disability. Folks, I'm here to tell you we all live a muddy life. Life is full of challenges, loss, meeting expectations, letting people down, being judged or being the one judging, feeling guilty, fighting illness . . . the list goes on and on.

We were all born to do something great with our life. Do not take for granted or discredit your gifts. Do not fall into the mud traps that hinder who you really are and who you want to become.

Always remember we are eternal divine spiritual beings living a temporary physical existence, and through the lessons, gratefulness, and authenticity, **you can max out your life through the mud!**

About Ruth and Mason

RUTH GRANT-BAILEY has been an RN for over thirty years, with most of her career experience in leadership and management. She brought an intensive physical therapy model to the Cincinnati area and co-founded a local intensive physical therapy center that treated children with neuromuscular disorders. Ruth also started two non-profits—Smiles for Kids and CP Inspires (no longer in place). These accomplishments, along with her strong advocacy for Mason and his medical care and treatments, led to her being recognized as one of Nabisco's 100 Extraordinary Women in 2018.

In addition to *A Muddy Life,* Ruth has written two children's books and several articles for various magazines. As an educator on cerebral palsy and intensive therapy models, she has done multiple presentations and speaking engagements at elementary schools, physician offices, PTA meetings, and chambers of commerce.

MASON BAILEY is a self advocate who owns and operates his own business, Seasonal Impact, and was certified in heavy equipment operating in 2019. He is a speaker and educator on cerebral palsy and how to treat those with disabilities and has spoken at elementary schools, county workshops, and medical residency programs.

In 2023, Mason was awarded the Al Miller Award for Gratitude by The Holocaust and Humanity Center in Cincinnati. He has also been featured on local news channels and in *My Life* magazine.

Learn more at RGBbooks.com.